LEVEL 42

LEVEL 42

The Definitive Biography

SIDGWICK & JACKSON
LONDON

First published in Great Britain in 1989 by
Sidgwick & Jackson Limited

ISBN 0-283-99837-7

Typeset by Hewer Text Composition Services, Edinburgh
Printed by Mackays of Chatham PLC, Chatham, Kent
for Sidgwick & Jackson Limited
1 Tavistock Chambers, Bloomsbury Way,
London WC1A 2SG

Contents

*To my parents for their faith, and to my wife
Diane and daughters, Stephanie and Hannah, for
whom I sincerely hope a better future might
not be a mere dream.*

Acknowledgements

I am indebted to many people for both their frankness and guidance during the writing of this biography. Foremost of these are the band members, both present and past. My thanks to Mike Lindup, Phil Gould and Boon Gould who willingly allowed me into their homes and subsequently into their minds, and for remembering all the small but important details. My thanks also to Boon for providing me with copious notes on his and Mark King's visit to the United States. And to Mark, whose management, after months of possibly, probably and definitely maybe, eventually made it possible for me to slot into a frantic work schedule long enough to be splendidly entertained by his life story with appropriate anecdotes to lighten the load.

My sincere gratitude goes to my Editor at Sidgwick & Jackson, Karen Hurrell, who sold the idea on my behalf to the publishers, and whose patience and unswerving enthusiasm since the very beginning saw me through many trying times, particularly when I explained that I could not meet the original deadline for the project. Thanks also for not attaching too many conditions as to the style or content.

Special thanks are extended to my sister Michelle and her husband Graham Edmunds for providing me with a bed, good food, and the space and solitude to put it all together, for willingly burning the candle at both ends in order to guide me through the bad patches, and for delicately, but emphatically, correcting my errors, both grammatical and geographical, during my hectic periods at the keyboard. You were both an inspiration.

Thank you to Ray and Bridget King for a most enjoyable time on the Isle of Wight, for answering so honestly my probing questions, for the loan of the cherished scrapbooks and for allowing me access to Mark's letters home. This book would not have been the same without your help. Neither would it have been without Nadia Cattouse for the fond recollections of her son Mike Lindup's childhood.

A band will always feel safe in the hands of a tour manager like Roger Searle. I chased him down in Gothenburg, Rome, Barcelona and London and, despite dealing with a multitude of matters, he always spared the time to chat. Thank you, Roger.

Among countless others, I would like to expressly mention Sue Venables, Graham Smith, Julie Brown and Pam Mennell, for both organizing and providing me with the transcripts from weeks of tape-recorded interviews; Verdine White of Earth, Wind And Fire for recollections of 1983; Lee Leschasin, Head of Press at Polydor Records; Linda McCartney for the back cover photograph; Simon Brodbeck at the *Daily Express*, who so willingly – and so often – re-adjusted the rotas to accommodate my research and writing spells; Wally Badarou; Alan Sizer; Sara Silver; Paul Fenn; and Andy Sojka. To those I have failed to mention, I apologize, but you have my personal gratitude.

Prologue

After five gruelling, non-stop touring years, by 1985 Level 42 were still perceived as a middle order, second division band. Having endured the long, often hard, learning process, they were undoubtedly successful but their popularity was not growing. Touring had proved to be their strongest selling point but not enough people were buying the records. The band were beginning to stagnate.

If anyone was to champion their cause, it had to be Mark King. He had emerged from being just one of four to the main one of four. Throughout his career he had had a burning desire to succeed and a total belief in what he was doing. In 1983, Verdine White, who alongside partner Larry Dunn of Earth, Wind And Fire had produced Level 42's album *Standing in the Light*, told Mark: 'When an artist has a hit it's a smash, but when a popular artist has a hit it's a smash smash!' If things didn't change soon, thought Mark, the band would end up with a posthumous hit.

As the New Year broke, Mark, Mike Lindup, and the brothers Boon and Phil Gould, in the presence of another Gould brother, John – Level 42's manager – sat round a table and asked themselves: 'Are we really happy?' Having been playing the same venues to the same sized audiences year in, year out, the answer was obvious and uncalled for. They needed hit records to herald new albums. They needed to play bigger venues. It wasn't simply a question of growing in popularity in Europe but of expanding their fan base in America. They desperately needed to break across the Atlantic.

Since 1980, Level 42 had been appearing under the Brit-funk umbrella, stabled with other acts such as Shakatak and Linx. The band, Polydor Records and the management knew that a change was necessary to catapult them more into the public eye. The problem was finding the right solution. They certainly couldn't turn to the Press for support, for although the band were liked on an individual level, they were thought of as pretty awful in a live situation with their soul-boy image. They didn't have funny haircuts and weren't in the teeny mould, so therefore they had no direct appeal to those in the 12–16-year-old bracket. The band had ridden to popularity as punk had died away. Unfortunately the latter scene had left a legacy whereby excellent musicianship was somewhat frowned upon. Being perceived as musicians' musicians was not a good thing. Outfits like Return To Forever and Spyro Gyra, however brilliant they may have been, were not huge money earners.

Half of Level 42's breaks had come because other people in the business had revered them. The fact that Mark was acknowledged as possibly the best bass player in the world was of no consequence. In fact the man himself has always been dismissive of such personal accolades. 'I find it flattering that I have taken on the mantle of being the new bass guitar hero but I am not overly sure that I warrant such praise,' he once told me. 'I have never gone through that old British tradition of having to suffer first for the sake of my art. I am certainly not precious about my studying the bass.'

It was clear what needed to be done – a change of musical direction, a slight touch on the writing tiller. As a result, the album *World Machine* made its grand exit from the studio. They had got it right. Level 42 had been commercial on their own terms and, despite popular opinion, there had been no deliberate compromise or sell-out. They had merely shifted gear and become more streamlined in the pop vein. 'The success of that album was like the final seal of approval for the band,' Mark told me after the hugely successful world tour that followed its release. 'Our success had been growing in strength and we had decided to try something different, hoping that we wouldn't offend our hard-core fans. We knew the risk there was in producing more commercial numbers but we wanted to appeal to a broader audience. The formula worked. We were at the stage where if it hadn't, *World Machine* might well have been the last album we made.'

Of course a certain fan element was mortally offended by Level 42's change of musical style. The band undoubtedly lost fans, but they also gained an awful lot more into the bargain. As manager Paul Crockford believes: 'The sort of people who used to like Level 42 but don't like them now are those who won't buy records if they are released in England but will buy them if they are US imports. It was a big cult thing about Level 42 being *their* little band. It's okay telling your mates about your little band, but when your mates also know about them, it's not the same. There's always a hard-core element with any *fans* who are involved from the beginning. They think the best thing since sliced bread is for the band to play one night at the Marquee in London. As soon as they play London's Hammersmith Odeon they think that "popular" means "sold out". Obviously the band changes. If you listen to the first album [*Level 42*], *Love Games*, and you listen to *Running in the Family*, they are a world apart, but they are both Level 42 records. The band has changed, and the fans either come along with you or they don't.'

Lyricist and drummer Phil Gould, however, was unable to adopt this pragmatic view since it contradicted all his musical ideals. Like some of the fans, he strongly objected to the sudden change in direction. The band, he felt, had lost its credibility in the market. Mark had been driving the machine and everyone else pretty much had gone along with it to date. His dominant personality had won the battle of wills. But suddenly Phil didn't trust his friend's judgement. Mark's burgeoning commercial sense rankled with him. It took the powers that be and Mike Lindup to dispel the immediate doubts, although they continued to bubble under the surface for Phil.

Paul Crockford, newly into the fold as manager, outlined to the band what he felt had been their problem since 1980 — namely, that they had never spent any money on presentation. The members had been conscious of the fact that an appropriate image had always been lacking. In fact what little projection they gave had always been barely functional, although the live shows had always gone down well. 'Let's go out and look expensive. Let's put on a proper show,' exclaimed Paul. They had never taken the risk before. Their shows had always been somewhat workmanlike. Now it was time to speculate.

No matter what reservations they may have had at the time, it was a fitting testament to their skills as musicians and to the fact that as an ensemble they were prepared to don a more creative hat that it worked. Level 42's live shows have since been described as the biggest disco in the world. The audience is guaranteed a good time. It may come across to some elements of the Press as being somewhat vacuous, but the band are not talking about changing the world.

They love performing live and have been one of the hardest-working bands on the road, averaging up to 100 shows a year. The 'Running in the Family' tour extended to over thirteen months and, as it transpired, saw the departure of both Phil and Boon Gould half-way through. With replacement musicians, Mark and Mike marched on. Mark at one point commented that the only way he knew what year it was, was that at one time they played an extra night at the Hammersmith Odeon and now they were playing an extra night at Wembley Arena.

If Level 42 had not made the decision in 1985 to change musical direction, it is unlikely they would be so venerated today. It has been a hard road but one which in the long run has borne fruit. Ironically, far from receding, the pressure that they have endured for so long has increased – along with their international status.

In such a volatile industry, no one can be certain of a band's longevity or continued success. For Mark King, a self-confessed workaholic, not for one second did he consider giving up. Since childhood music has been one long love affair.

Chapter One
Island of dreams

As you look out from Cowes on the Isle of Wight over the Solent
on a bright summer's day, and your eyes feast on a plethora
of sail, it is easy to understand why people over the centuries
have regarded the United Kingdom as a nation of seafarers. The
brightly-coloured spinnakers of the racing yachts billow in the
wind, and solo sailors in their dinghies vie for precious space
with their more able-bodied fellows on Britain's most popular
stretch of sailing water.

It is against this delightful backdrop that Raymond King was
raised. His mother, Alice, came from Portsmouth on England's
south coast and Edward, his father, was from farming stock. Ray's
grandmother was one of thirteen children. Upon marriage, as a
wedding present each was given a farm on the Isle of Wight, so
that at one time in the not-too-distant past the Kings owned a
sizeable chunk of the Island. As mechanization costs increased, so
too the farms grew to become unviable and were slowly but surely
broken up and sold. Only five currently remain in the family.

Ray King had no interest in or intention of taking up this tough
existence when the time came for him to leave school and seek
employment. Instead he went into boat-building, joining the
John Samuel Whites shipyard in Cowes. Ray served a five-year
apprenticeship from the age of 15 to 20, but subsequently became
disillusioned and switched to the building industry where he
employed his skills as a carpenter.

Bridget Flux also came from a farming background and, as a child, would travel around the Island on carts visiting her friends. She first met Ray King in 1950 while visiting his uncle, Bill Downer, at Cliff Farm, near the village of Gurnard, west of Cowes. In their social life, they had little to do for enjoyment except dance, and Saturday nights were set aside for this. The main problem was transport, as the best dances were held at the Manor House on the other side of the Island – and they didn't own a car. As a result, they were occasionally given a lift by Tom Skeets, whose mother was Bill Downer's daughter. When getting to the dances proved too much of a problem, there was always the cinema on a Saturday morning, and Newport boasted three – the Medina, the Odeon and the Grand – so Ray and Bridget were at least able to go out together regularly.

On 28 August 1953, Ray and Bridget married. They were 19 and 17 years old respectively. Ray at this time was serving his apprenticeship as a boat-builder living in the village of Northwood but, the nuptials over, he and his new bride moved in to 'Jamesbridge', Rew Street, Gurnard, the bungalow owned by Bridget's mother Margaret. On 4 March of the following year, the Kings' first daughter, Belinda Mary, was born, and the family moved to 'Thorness View', Northwood. The farmhouse was part of Kingswell Dairy, a farm owned by another of Ray's uncles. On 2 July 1955, baby Rachel Ann came into the world.

Their brother Mark weighed in at 9lb on 20 October 1958 at 'Thorness View'. Bridget remembers it as a painful delivery, particularly as the birth of her daughters had gone so smoothly. By this time Ray had completed his apprenticeship as a boat-builder and was employed by Ron Westbrook, a well-known builder from Cowes. It wasn't long before Ray realized that being rained on, and being rained off, was not for him, so he took a drop in pay and joined the prison service. He was seeking a job with security, although he was prepared to set aside any thoughts of promotion in order to stay on the Island. 'My family was on the Island, and Bridget's family was here, and I wasn't going to be made a gypsy of by travelling all over the country,' remembers Ray. In fact, a year after joining, there was a large pay award which took him over what he had been previously earning as a carpenter, so he felt sure he had made the right career decision. 'I wasn't sure at first, though, trying to scrape along and bring up three children. But it has given us good security and I've never been unemployed in my life.'

The move was still a wrench for Ray, though, as he got on well with Ron Westbrook and enjoyed sailing with Ron's two sons. But the thought of ending up at sixty-five as a carpenter didn't impress him. 'Thorness View' was pretty basic, and the prison service was offering a pension, early retirement and free housing. On reflection, it wasn't that hard a decision to make. 'After applying, the whole Westbrook family was gathered in the main office,' says Ray. 'They called me in and asked if I wasn't happy working with them, as they had received notice from the Home Office that I had applied to join the service. I told them I just wanted to try something else. In the end they said that if things didn't work out after my year's probationary period, my old job would still be waiting for me.'

It was December 1960. The first three months were hard and Ray wasn't sure that he could handle the work. After all, locking people up for a living and not reacting to that situation in the initial stages is hard, and he wasn't sure he would shape up to his fellow officers. It's a complete shock to the system, switching from a loving family environment to prison, with its smells and the undercurrent of violence. Ray handled it and eventually slotted in. But if it was hard for Ray, it was even tougher on Bridget, left at home with three children in the bleak mid-winter with no central heating at 'Thorness View', and Ray away on his three-month induction course. Belinda and Rachel went down with measles and toddler Mark had a streaming cold. Ray returned home one weekend to find his two lovely daughters covered from head to toe in spots. Fortunately, help was not far away, with Ray's parents living opposite. His father would often pop across the road in the early hours of the morning to make sure Ray was up and ready for work. He always was and can boast a clean record for punctuality over twenty-eight years.

Mark's earliest recollections of his childhood are linked with tractors on the farm at Kingswell Dairy. 'It was never a big working farm and I can remember going down to the end of the garden one day when I was about two years old to ride on the tractor. It was such a long trip that by the time I reached the tractor I had made a mess in my pants. I felt really annoyed that having gone all the way there and climbing on board I ended up doing that. By the time I arrived back home again my grandparents had arrived and I remember feeling incredibly embarrassed at my mum changing me in front of them.'

He also has vivid memories of being bathed in the sink. Bridget would polish the large brass tap and Mark remembers that if you put your face close to it, your reflection was like Pete Townshend of the Who – although Mark didn't know it at the time.

Because of the farm environment, grandfather King would buy toddler Mark plastic pigs and cattle, and toy tractors as presents. He loved to play around the farm and had a red pedal-car that Bridget and Ray would place on the front of an upturned table so their son could pretend he was on a float in a carnival procession.

From 'Thorness View' to the prison was a journey of about two miles and Ray would travel by motorbike. In order to improve their social life and be among people of their own age, the King family moved into prison quarters at 53 Standen Avenue, Camphill, in 1961. A year later they switched to 15 Crossways, Camphill, which is in a beautiful spot on the edge of Parkhurst Forest.

One of the Kings' neighbours was prison barber Bob Coggins, who would give Mark a 'number one' haircut. Mark remembers: 'Once a month on a Sunday I would go round to the house; a tablecloth would be tied around my neck and I would be given this haircut. My head used to be shaved and I would end up looking like someone out of *World At War*.' The prisoners nicknamed the short-cropped blond Mark 'Butch'. They also had another name for him – 'Noddy'. 'We used to have a dog called Shandy which had distemper and she used to nod her head because of it,' remembers Mark. 'One day she mysteriously died. I've since learned that my grandfather took her up to the forest and knocked her on the head with a shovel. I also remember my sister Belinda saying to me, "Shandy's dead and you don't care". She was forcing out the tears and I didn't understand what she was saying.'

From Crossways, the young Mark would walk to the prison and stand at the gates. When the working parties returned they would take him inside and stand him in the gatehouse where he would dance the Twist on the table for them. Ray would not be overly impressed by this but Mark would always have an excuse up his sleeve for being there to meet his father after work.

Because of the age gap between Mark and his two sisters, Belinda and Rachel would often use their little brother for their games when they lived at Northwood, dressing him up and using him as a live doll in their pram. He was quite happy to play along with them, as it was about the only form of companionship he had at the time.

At the age of five Mark started at Parkhurst Infants and Primary School, continuing there for four years before he joined the Junior School. As he hadn't attended a nursery first, he didn't take well to his first taste of school. But at least at Camphill he had the opportunity to mix with children of his own age. The officers' children could play in safety around the estate roads because they were free of traffic apart from staff vehicles.

Mark, Belinda and Rachel also attended a local Sunday school run by a Mr and Mrs Marks, where young Mark became involved in nativity plays and would dress as an angel – even if at times he wasn't one. But he had his rabbits and dogs and cats at home to play with, so his was a happy childhood. One thing he didn't enjoy, though, was Sunday school; in fact he hated it. 'We used to have school in the front room of the Marks's house, where we would be made to take our shoes off. One day I had a hole in my sock and Mrs Marks told everyone to look at it. That put me off older women!'

While at Camphill, in 1966, Ray and Bridget fostered a baby girl, Anna Marie. They quickly became attached and Ray made tentative inquiries about adoption but within days the child had been taken away from them. Undeterred, the Kings then fostered a four-year-old girl, Jackie Brown, who fell into the family scene very quickly and would enjoy playing with the Kings' three children. But she was never happier than on those Sunday mornings when her father would arrive to take her out.

Ray spent seven years at Camphill. Towards the end of his

time there he would accompany parties of prisoners preparing the ground for the erection of Albany Prison. He liked the idea of moving to a new prison environment and, as a consequence, the family moved to 17 Argyle Road, Albany, in March 1967. In fact the house was only a stone's throw from their previous residence, but it was a different housing section and place of work. Most of Mark's friends had been from the Island but upon the move to Albany, he was surrounded by northerners – Geordies, Mancunians and Liverpudlians – whose accents he found it hard to understand.

Mark began at the newly-built Parkhurst County Junior School in September, 1967, where he joined the football team and became an active member of Newport Boxing Club. He was small for his age but was not afraid to go charging in when necessary. He played football at left-back. In fact his prowess on the field earned him a forward line position in an Island Inter-Schools Cup competition, where he and his team-mates each won a medal.

'I always prefered boxing to football because I used to hate getting cold hands, stood out in freezing weather on a wet field on a Saturday morning. Playing at number three with my shaved head, I used to go around kicking people's shins and acting very tough. I made the trials for the Island football team, which at the time seemed like a great honour, until I didn't make the team and then I put them down to being a bunch of woofters, like you do!'

Mark was also proving to be a tough contestant in the boxing ring, and fought for his school in the Isle of Wight Amateur Boxing Association competitions. Although he says he didn't do particularly well in the ring, he did win three trophies. It was usually real hell-for-leather stuff.

Mark often came up against a tough opponent from Ryde called John Derry who would always manage to beat him. In the final of what proved to be Mark's last competitive bout, there was young Derry again in the opposite corner. Mark led with his right and dropped his hand at what proved to be the wrong moment. He caught a nasty blow which knocked one of his knuckles back but, true to form, he courageously fought on, virtually taking the fight to the final bell with one hand. He lost on points, collecting a runner's-up medal. Ray remembers: 'These two boys looked so angelic with their short, blond hair, but they could really fight. It was unbelievable to see two ten-year-olds battling it out so hard.' After the fight, Mark decided to hang up his gloves, preferring to concentrate on the less dangerous pursuit of acquiring musical knowledge.

'I used to go to Newport Boxing Club on Thursday nights. When I look back on it now, I think I could have been so much better at it,' admits Mark. 'At the time, because I was a bit lazy, I suppose, I never used to enjoy it very much. It was always a hassle and I used to look forward to the tea break. If it did what dad wanted it to do – and that was toughen me up – then it succeeded in that. I don't ever remember being bullied at school. After the boxing club stint, I could certainly look after myself. Because of the schools connection, any awards would be presented during assembly, and for the rest of the week after an award ceremony you would have someone coming up and saying, "So you think you're tough, do you?" You would then have a fight.'

If Mark was good at sport, he proved only an average scholar. He wasn't fond of school, and lived for the school discos and plays in which he would become actively involved. Each morning for breakfast he would eat cornflakes with warm milk and on the way to school would be sick in the hedge. 'I think it was more nerves than anything else. I always seemed to be quite tense at school. I used to think, thank goodness for weekends, it's two days off from being sick. My receptiveness to learning isn't that bad. Unfortunately you have to do it at your own speed. Figures are something that seem to frighten everybody but they shouldn't because they are only squiggles on a page. It's school that puts you in this frame of mind. You learn as a child that if you ask too many questions, you're not thought of as being bright, but stupid. Schools don't breed individuals, they breed uniformity. That rears its ugly head when eventually you leave home and do your own thing. You return to see your mates, those that never stepped out of the uniformity, and they hate you for it. I saw it a couple of years ago with old friends that I had been so close at school with who now seemed almost aggressive towards me.'

Chapter Two
Drum crazy

It soon became obvious that Mark had talent as a musician, even if at times it drove his parents crazy. He would often sit at the table banging away with his knife and fork while waiting for Bridget to serve the meal. If it was a miserable, wet day, he would get out the saucepans and play them. Biscuit tin lids and pickle jars were also favoured because they made such a good sound.

Enough is enough, thought Ray King, we get the hint. Although neither he nor Bridget knew one musical instrument from another, both could see Mark's enthusiasm and potential and, in 1968, Ray splashed out £10 on their son's first drum kit. Mark had seen it advertised and Ray said he would check it out. If it was any good, he would buy it. 'You wouldn't think that at nine years of age you would ask somebody, "Do you know where I can get a drum kit?"' recalls Mark. 'I can vividly remember being told that the man in Newport who lived in the house with the threepenny bit windows had a kit for sale. I walked all the way there and made the inquiry. It had an enormous, thin bass drum, the type you see in carnivals, with a single-headed tom-tom and a thin snare drum that was almost like a tambourine with two heads. When you hit the brass cymbals they would dent into a new shape. All the stands came out of the bass drum. I saw this kit and I thought it was fantastic. I think because I had made the effort to go and look at it, dad said I could have it. I didn't know anything about the fact that it was really expensive, especially then, and that dad wasn't earning that much money. You don't think about things like that at that age.

'We bought it and I told Mrs Drudge, the music teacher and also my form teacher at Parkhurst Junior School, about the kit, and I would take it to school. I remember going to Carisbrooke High School (now Secondary School) to take part in this piece called *The Little Drummer Boy*. The children stood and did their parts, and then someone said, "And here he is, the star of our show, Mark King", and I tapped out this beat on the kit. It went down really well and that night at home, lying in front of the electric fire, I kept saying to mum and dad when they had stopped talking about it, "It was great, though, wasn't it?" It was such an enormous success that we had to perform it in assembly. Unfortunately, before the show, the snare string broke and it ended up sounding like a tom-tom. I tried to tell Mrs Drudge my problem as she announced me, but she told me to carry on. Even at nine years of age I was very much aware that it didn't sound like a snare drum. So in the space of a week I had my first wonderful experience of elation through appearing in front of people, of being the centre of attention and of them being proud of me, and a disaster. It was all character-building stuff.'

Despite his disappointment, the majority of the time Mark was in his element, as his whole life at this time started to revolve around music. Whenever he had the kit at home, he would set it up in his bedroom which extended over the neighbour's passageway. They didn't complain, though, as they appreciated that this budding Buddy Rich was not just banging away for the sake of it. Even so, Ray was pleased that they were good friends.

As Mark's playing ability progressed, Ray was more than happy to dip his hand into his pocket again and buy his son a better kit. The red Pearl set from Teagues music shop in Newport set Ray back £109. It was a fortune in those days to spend on such a young lad, but his parents knew he was worth it, even if others looked upon Mark as a spoilt brat. 'It wasn't a case of that,' says Ray. 'I knew that Mark was no academic, but I also knew that he could make a living out of music and a brand new drum kit would help him to improve his playing.'

It was around this time that the family attended a show in Ryde where a new range of Premier drum kits were on display. Mark and Ray sat in the audience and listened to a talk on how wonderful the kits were before the speaker asked if anyone wanted to try out a set. It was all eager-beaver Mark needed. He leapt up and charged to the front. 'Down he went and they were thinking, "Who's this little squirt?" and "Be careful, don't damage it",' recalls Ray. 'But he got up there and made the fellow who was demonstrating look third-rate. That's when Teagues took an interest in him. The owner came and saw me afterwards and said that Mark was different from the average boy playing music and why didn't I take him into the shop. From then on I used to take him down there and he could play anything he wanted.'

Ray went on to buy Mark various guitars (Teagues even sent to America on a later occasion for a Fender Stratocaster which couldn't be bought in the country at the time). In 1969, at the age of 11, Mark started lessons on acoustic guitar with Tom Taylor, a gifted musician who was proficient on bass as well as six-stringed guitar. He lived in a small property called Blackwater Cottage in Newport, which has since been demolished. Ray would take Mark along on alternate Sunday mornings. Young Mark quickly excelled on lead and acoustic guitar and had a lovely touch, particularly on jazz numbers. Ray acquired a black Teasco guitar for £12 but later bought the Fender as Mark's ability grew.

Now there were the drums and the guitar playing to contend with in the King household. Every day when he arrived home from school Mark would head straight for his drum kit. Everything else took second place. It was practice, practice, practice. Even at school during lunch breaks he would not go out to play with his classmates. It was straight on to his old drum kit which he had 'sold' to Parkhurst School for £5. By this time Mark had his new Olympic kit waiting for him every time he walked through the front door at home. Mark always held that if you buy a cheap instrument, your music will sound cheap. Sound logic. 'We always tried to get him the best and that's why it sounded good. It's money well spent,' says Ray.

A stickler for documentation, Mark still has all his musical instruments and their prices listed in a diary: First drum kit £10,

Red Pearl kit £109; Fender £282; Teasco £15; Impact Amp £200; Olympic kit £115; Premier kit £420; Tape £80. He fully appreciated the outlay and sacrifices his father was making on his behalf, and was to repay the kindness as soon as he was able.

During 1969 Ray King spent three months with the Metropolitan Police to train as a dog handler. On his return he was assigned a large, short-haired Alsatian named Dax. The prison had an area specifically set aside for kennels but because the King family liked Dax so much, the dog stayed at their home. 'We didn't bring him completely into the family environment. He lived outside in the side passage to the house,' remembers Ray. Mark got to know Dax well and would often accompany his father and the dog during training sessions.

On Saturday nights Ray and Bridget King would visit the prison officers' club, but on the night of 11 October 1969, they had friends round for drinks. Dax was in his normal place in the outside passage, near to the outside toilet. Instead of using the inside toilet, Mark decided to go outside. It was a bad decision. Dax flew at him. The first thing the Kings and their friends knew about it was when Mark burst into the living room with blood streaming down his face. It was the first time his parents had heard him swear. 'Look what your bloody dog's just done to me!' he shouted. He dropped his hand and exposed a severe gash on his left cheek. Bridget was horrified. Mark's face was quickly wrapped in a towel and Ray headed off in his grey Ford Zodiac to St Mary's Hospital, Newport. Unfortunately there was no one around to attend to Mark, so they then made for St John's Hospital, Ryde, where Mark received sixteen stitches.

'I'm sure it was my fault. Dax was asleep and, being just a kid, I bent down and ruffled his head. He woke up, went silly and bit me,' recalls Mark. It was fortunate that he knew the commands. 'Dax! Leave!' he shouted, and the dog duly obeyed. But only for an instant. He attacked again, but this time Mark managed to put his arm in front of his face. So the dog bit that instead. Dax, it transpired, had been suffering from a brain tumour and Ray had to have him put down.

'It was awful. I just couldn't believe it,' says Ray. 'I dread to think what would have happened if we had decided to go out that Saturday evening. Poor Mark just stood there with his face gaping open.

'I always felt that if I had done what the department said and put the dog out in the kennels, it would never have happened. We didn't make a big song and dance about it. I could have made a complaint but then I felt that if they gave me a dog, it was my responsibility. They wanted to put me down for the next course with the Metropolitan Police, but I said no. That incident finished my career as a dog handler.'

If it affected Mark, he didn't let it show. The prison officers were extremely kind to him when they found out what had happened. They made a collection and he was spoilt whenever he visited the club.

It was the first bad thing that had happened to Mark, but it had little effect on him. When he eventually became a house owner, the first thing he did was buy an Alsatian puppy.

As his face slowly began to heal, it was obvious that the scars would be prominent, so Ray took Mark along to see a specialist, who duly asked him if he was at all bothered about it. 'It doesn't bother me. It's there,' was his reply. Asked if he wanted skin grafts to be carried out, Mark didn't know what to reply. The specialist told him that in days gone by in Germany, it was a sign of manhood to bear such a scar across one's face. That was all the excuse young Mark needed. No skin grafts, thank you. That's a duelling scar. It has never been touched since.

In 1970, when Mark was twelve, he formed his first live act – a duo with his friend Colin Gibson, the son of a prison officer who lived on the same estate. Mark played drums and Colin handled guitar and vocals. Their first big break almost happened for them when they attended an audition in Southampton for a children's television show called *Anything You Can Do*. Playing several numbers by the Beatles, they failed the audition – in fact they got pushed out of the running by a tap dancer! – but it certainly whetted Mark's appetite.

The duo often appeared at Albany Prison Officers' Club. They used to cause quite a stir with the members, and Ray remembers on one occasion they played at the club before some show-business personalities who had been involved in a Celebrity XI football match in Newport. Among the celebrities were DJ Ed Stewart and actress Ingrid Pitt. The lads also appeared at Little Canada, a Pontin's holiday camp.

On 29 August 1970, Mark's brother Nathan was born. It is doubtful whether the baby got much sleep, as Mark was still heavily engrossed in his music. In 1971 Ray bought him the Fender Stratocaster and an amplifier. Mark would disappear into his room after arriving home from school and re-appear several hours later absolutely exhausted. He would listen to records by the Rolling Stones and Cream – bass player Jack Bruce has always been a firm favourite of his – and learn the chord structures as he listened. He was also receiving music lessons at school. The problem he faced when drumming along with the radio was that half the time he couldn't hear what he was supposed to be playing because he was drowning himself out. Ray and Bridget solved that one by buying him some practice drum pads.

In 1971 Mark moved to Cowes High School. He would travel there either on the bus or by racing cycle. He was keen to expand his musical knowledge by learning to play the cello but the school did not allow that because he was already reading guitar music. He also had to be content with playing drums in the school orchestra.

He decided to join the school's Army Cadet Force where he could play drums. The only trouble was that he had no inclination for military-style playing. You name it, he could play it, as long as it wasn't regimented. 'I don't like that,' he would tell Ray. 'There's something funny about it.'

Ray spoke to the band leader, asking: 'I believe you've got problems with Mark and his drumming?'

'Trouble? You can say that again. Mark's supposed to be playing a set rhythm pattern and all he wants to do is the Ted Heath and Joe Loss stuff. I can't have that in a military band,' said Fred Penny, the leader.

So Mark did not stay long with them, although he did travel to France on a cadet trip. That also proved eventful. Going through the motions of a beached landing, young Mark, at the front as usual, was first off the landing craft with his imitation rifle. He jumped out and, because of his small stature, disappeared over the side and up to his neck in water. 'The Army's not for me, Dad,' he told Ray on his return.

His guitar teacher, Tom Taylor, was always telling Mark to join the Army where he would receive a good musical education. Ray was also approached on one occasion by a scout from the Royal Marines who had heard Mark play percussion and said that he could offer the boy a good future. Ray collected all the necessary literature but Mark had already been put off by his cadet misadventures.

Ray and Bridget were forever trying to get their elder son to think of what career he would like to pursue, but his head was so full of music that he could not think of anything else.

Chapter Three
King of the wild frontier

Ray King remembers being called to Cowes High School by Mark's head of department over his lack of concentration in the classroom. 'I had a serious word with Mark and told him he was getting into trouble with the school and asked why were things going wrong,' says Ray.

Mark replied: 'I've got music going through my head all the time. It's not that I'm not doing anything in class.'

Ray knew there was no point in shouting at his son because in some ways he understood and sympathized, but at the same time it did create a problem. The school complained that Mark was forever staring out into space instead of at the blackboard. His thoughts would still be with him when he arrived home from school, and Mark would set them down on the Grundig tape recorder Ray had bought for him. 'Even today in the music he is writing I can hear some of those thoughts he laid down on tape,' admits Ray.

In 1971, at the age of thirteen, Mark joined a group called Pseudo Foot who played cover versions of the pop music of the time. The group is still in existence today, with original members Annie and Martin Cave. Mark was brought in on drums and, although he hated it, he was also expected to sing. The bass guitar was played by Phil Whittington and on lead guitar was a friend called Dave Deacon, whose brother had been the previous drummer. At the time the Osmonds were at their peak and poor Mark, as his voice had not broken by then, was expected to sing 'Rockin' Robin' and 'Long-Haired Lover from Liverpool'. Even as a young schoolboy Mark was playing most nights of the week around the pub circuit and at venues like the Gurnard Hotel, the Woodvale Hotel and various holiday camps. Mark was in great demand, even though he was still a minor. He was expected to play on Sunday lunchtimes at the *Ryde Queen*. He also appeared on board the *Medway Queen*, a former paddle steamer then set in concrete. The steamer played a large part in the evacuation of Dunkirk during the Second World War. A disco was held aboard downstairs, and Pseudo Foot appeared upstairs. The *Medway Queen* has since returned to the River Medway, where she received her name.

The *Islander* newspaper was to write of Pseudo Foot in February 1973: 'This able five-piece possesses a pleasant not too noisy sound that goes down well with all age groups, teen and twenty, mum and dad, and even gran and grandpa. Basically, it is a form of poppy-folk, not unlike that which is performed by the New Seekers. Jangling lead and rhythm guitars provide a splendid backing to the sweet, well-controlled vocals, and superb, wandering bass guitar work provides amazing depth to the whole. Also, well worth listening to is the drumming of pint-sized percussionist Mark King. Just fourteen-years-old, and with the ability of a professional.'

'Pseudo Foot was great,' says Mark. 'I enjoyed it immensely, mainly because of Phil Whittington, who was such a good bass player. He was a real hero of mine. He was a good singer, although he never used to sing in the group. He was also good at arm wrestling, and used to drive around in a three-wheeler. I was in Pseudo Foot during the Mod days, and he would dress in a parka.'

The headmaster at Cowes found out that Mark was appearing in public houses and other venues. 'I can't exactly remember whether we told Mark he had to stop playing with Pseudo Foot,' Ray says, 'but I know the school felt that it just wasn't on, so Mark stopped. If he wasn't appearing with Pseudo Foot, he was playing with someone else.' Mark's time was also taken up with the Isle of Wight School Orchestra, with whom he would practise on Saturday mornings.

'I used to earn a small fortune and I don't understand what I used to spend it all on. From the age of eleven I never had problems earning money,' says Mark. 'I would earn £2 on Friday nights and £3 on Saturdays playing at the Gurnard Hotel. The taxman clobbered me for about £160 when I left school for earning when I was a pupil.

'Mr Marr, the German teacher and year tutor, told mum and dad that I should stop these activities. What annoyed the school was the fact that I would see the teachers in the Gurnard Hotel on a Friday night. It must have ruined their evening no end to have their entertainment laid on by the boy that they were probably shouting at the same afternoon in class.'

In February 1972, the King family moved to 'Jamesbridge', Rew Street, Gurnard, to look after Bridget's mother. At that time the bungalow was quite small (Ray has since had it extended) and it was quite an upheaval when they moved. Ray had to buy a caravan for sisters Belinda and Rachel to live in, and Mark and his brother Nathan had to share a room with Mark's drums. As soon as the girls left home, Mark took over the caravan as a practice room. He pinned up an old shawl, which had slightly Indian overtones to it, on the ceiling, and burned joss sticks. With £25 in his pocket, he set off for Southsea and in Laskys electrical shop bought an Amstrad 2000 amplifier. He retrieved two old speakers from a school dustbin and built cabinets for them and, with his Garrard SP25 MkIV turntable completing the makeshift stereo outfit, would invite his girlfriends round to listen to music.

Young Mark used to play some terrible tricks on granny Margaret. 'When I was about thirteen, one of my school friends, Clive Martin, and I used to experiment with Clan Dew, a blend of wine and whisky. We would get drunk and go whizzing round the garden at all hours of the night. My mum and dad didn't know anything about it because we were very quiet round their side of the house. We used to knock on granny's window. Clive had a candle on the end of a stick. I would get my bicycle pump, fill it with petrol and pump it at the candle. This ball of flame would shoot across the window. Granny would end up chasing us round the garden with a frying pan and the next day would tell mum that she had had the strangest dream.' Boys will be boys.

Mark would also be terrible to his pet hamster. Amazed that hamsters' feet are very similar to human hands, it didn't take him long to discover that you can hang a hamster on a washing line. If you pinged the line, the animal would hang on by one 'hand'.

Brother Nathan would sometimes get the rough end of Mark's pranks. On one occasion Mark made a 'goat-kart' with a couple of pram wheels, an orange box and a wooden shaft on either side which were used as handles to pull the kart. He would harness one of his pet goats to the shafts and sit a bewildered two-year-old Nathan in the box. Says Mark: 'Understandably, if you place a stick between the back legs of a goat and waggle it around, the animal is going to freak out. That's what I used to do, and can they move! Nathan's face was a treat to behold. Many was the time the goat-kart would finish upside down, with Nathan still inside.'

There was no rest for poor Nathan, even in bed. Mark had a passion for the Pan horror books, which had hideous drawings on the front covers. Nathan couldn't relax with one of the books in their room, so thoughtful brother Mark would leave one on the pillow of his bunk bed. Nathan would scream and Mark would get it in the neck from his parents. But he got his own back. He put a blank cassette in his player and wound it on close to the end of one side, where he recorded some haunting voices. While Bridget was brushing Nathan's teeth, Mark rewound the tape and set it running under the bed. About forty-five minutes later there was a loud scream from the bedroom and Nathan came rushing into the lounge shouting: 'Mum, Mark's in there!' Innocent-looking Mark, of course, was sitting on the settee between his parents complaining that his younger brother was continually trying to get him into trouble. Nathan received a spanked bottom and was sent to bed.

Because of his name, Mark had a couple of nicknames doing the rounds. Sometimes he would be called Joe because he was always laughing (Joe King), and during his drumming phases he was Marking (Mark King) Time. Mark was in great demand for his percussive skills, because he enjoyed playing kettle drums. But even here he would do his own thing. Complimentary letters would still find their way to the King household, though.

Charles Shaw, conductor of the Dunford Orchestra, wrote: 'Dear Mark, Just to thank you again for your great help in our recent concert, not only for your fine playing (well, apart from some slightly weird departures from the score in the *Neil Courtney*, but only the composer, myself and you would know that, wouldn't *they*!).' Mark slipped in little naughties which he thought added to the piece but it was all part of the learning process, and young Mark was learning extremely fast. It was growing increasingly obvious where his major talent lay, and how his career would fan out.

Ray and Bridget spent much of their time ferrying Mark around the Island, to theatres in Sandown and Shanklin, with the large kettle drums as additional passengers. 'Obviously, at fourteen and fifteen he was too young to transport himself. He had to have mum and dad do it for him,' says Ray. 'It's a good job we had a motor car or his career would have been greatly restricted.

'He could play parts in *Choral Fantasia* and pieces like that, but I wouldn't say he liked it. Then again, he didn't exactly dislike it. The violinists would never stray from the score, yet they loved Mark because he injected something more into the music. His pitch was perfect. It was just a gift, I suppose. You've either got it or you haven't. The Isle of Wight School Orchestra was a great grounding for Mark to have had, teaching him stage presence and having the best teachers around you. He was very fortunate.'

Mark's music teacher at Cowes High School was Graham Holmes, with whom he had a good relationship. He used to visit Ray at the prison, where he taught music, and would say: 'You've got a very exceptional son, you know. I don't know whether you're aware of it. He's going to be very, very big one day.' He was right. 'I've taught him all I know,' he told Ray. 'And now he's got to get out in the world and do it himself.'

In 1972 sister Belinda left for Canada to become an au pair. Rachel was the next one to fly the family nest, leaving the caravan free for Mark to take over. At this time, as well as Pseudo Foot, he was playing with the Savoyards and the Dunford Orchestra. This was possibly a more serious period for Mark, when he decided he wanted to learn piano. He appreciated the fact that although he could read guitar music, it would help him enormously if he could also master piano music. Bridget went with Mark to talk to the head of music on the Isle of Wight at the County Hall to see how Mark could enter music college. 'He shattered our dreams because he said Mark would have to have at least Grade 8 on the piano, and Mark was quite disillusioned because he only had achieved Grade 1 at this stage. I don't know why we didn't push the guitar because he could read guitar music. He said there wasn't much hope of Mark getting to college at that stage,' she remembers. The lesson they learnt from that was that they started Nathan on piano lessons at the age of four. The irony is that today you can get into music college to study percussion, something you couldn't do in Mark's day.

In 1973, aged fifteen, Mark played the part of the boy in the Cowes High School production of *The Best Years Of Our Lives*, with the teachers playing the main parts. It was at this time that he also acquired a new silver Premier drum kit, which set Ray back £420. The Kings still have it to this day and Nathan often picks up the drumsticks. The following year Mark got a job at Somerton Garage, Northwood, serving petrol at weekends. He started paying his dad back for the Premier drum kit around this time. Ray remembers: 'I got hit badly for tax. I didn't think a schoolboy had to declare that he was working, and what with playing music and pumping petrol he did. They clobbered me for a lot of money.' When Mark was out playing, he had to get someone to stand in for him on the pumps.

In 1975 the CSE examinations loomed large. Mark sat History, Maths, Religious Studies and French, and received grades 4, 3, 4 and 4 respectively. After the exams were over, he joined Alan Dale, a singer and pianist, on the drums for a summer season. Alan, a North Country lad who could fill any place, is still performing today around the camps. It was a long summer season, as Ray and Bridget had to take Mark out every night to Fairway Park Holiday Camp at Sandown. He was receiving the grand total of £5 a night for his efforts.

In the same year Ray's father retired and the family held a surprise party at which Mark took centre-stage for the singalongs. At all the family get-togethers Mark would pick up the acoustic guitar and entertain. When he was younger, Mark would often sing with Ray's sister Jean's two children.

While living on the Albany estate in 1975, Mark would often give drum tuition to other officers' children for pocket money. Mark definitely set a trend. Because the officers saw what it was possible for another officer's son to do in the clubs if he had flair, they would buy instruments for their respective children. Mark later gave tuition in the caravan at Gurnard.

There were several talented officers at Albany who formed a group called the Yorkies (they were aged between 25 and 35), but they were short of a bass player. Mark was playing lead guitar at the time. A colleague of Ray's, Barry Bigby, said one day: 'Do you think Mark could show me a few things because I want to get in the band?' He duly spent some time with Mark having tuition. Although Mark had not picked up a bass before this time, he went up and down the fretboard with such dexterity that Barry couldn't believe his eyes. Whatever Mark picked up he could play.

He had bought a musty old piano for £25 while having private lessons. There he was in a bedroom with brother Nathan, a set of drums and a piano. 'He wasn't very popular!' confides Bridget. 'Although he only had a short time learning the piano, taking just the Grade 1 exam, he didn't seem to be practising much to me so I told him we couldn't afford to pay for the lessons if he wasn't going to bother. So he stopped going.'

Bridget's mother died in the spring of 1976, which left one room empty in the house. Around the same time Mark passed his driving test. Two days after his success, he asked Ray if he could take his girlfriend for a drive. Ray was happy to oblige and off Mark drove in the family's newly-acquired Austin Allegro. Driving by La Babalu club near Ryde Airport on a quiet, misty night, correctly on his side of the road, a taxi, travelling in the opposite direction, apparently pulled across the road in front of him and wrote the car off. Mark's girlfriend, Susan Lloyd, came off the worse of the two. She smashed into the windscreen and broke her jaw. The fact that she was wearing a seat belt saved her from going through the windscreen, but unfortunately she was wearing a ring with raised edges. Her hand was resting on the dashboard and as she was thrown forward with the momentum of the crash, the ring slashed her face. As for Mark, there was not a scratch on him. 'I would much rather it had been the other way round,' he says. Mark later purchased his own car, a Ford Escort.

In June 1976 Mark sat his O Level examinations in English Language, English Literature and Physics. He achieved grades of B, E and E respectively. In the autumn he returned to school, but it was obvious from the outset that his heart wasn't in it. He left without finishing the first term. He told his parents: 'I want to play music. If I don't go now, I'm going to dip out. I'll be playing holiday camps around the Isle of Wight for the rest of my life.'

Mark tried his hand at the Ronson factory near Newport in the autumn for a few months after he left school. He worked on the line making cigarette lighters. Jobs were starting to become difficult to find at this time but he didn't stay there long. He kept saying that he wanted to be a musician but he didn't want to stay on the Island and play. Ray was forever trying to encourage him to get a job during the day and play music in the evenings, because then he would lead a better life style than anybody else. 'I didn't envisage things like they are now. I just knew he had a talent and I wanted him to use it. But he had other ideas about the way he wanted to approach it. We tried to get him to join the police force but he wasn't going to do that. It finished up that instead of Mark joining the police, Belinda, upon her return from Canada, joined the prison service and served as an officer for eight-and-a-half years at Holloway. So instead of my son following in my footsteps, my elder daughter did. Mark just wanted to do music,' says Ray.

Both Belinda and Mark were in fact out of work at the beginning of 1977. In the March, Bridget heard of a job going as a milkman with Joe Butcher in Rew Street, whom Bridget's father had previously worked for. Mark started his rounds and also took on some farm work. He got on well with Don, Joe's son. Belinda joined the prison service in the May. The following month Mark became an uncle when his other sister, Rachel, gave birth to baby Anna. When Belinda finished her training in Essex she transferred to Holloway and, suddenly, the family had someone in London with their own flat. At last Mark had somewhere to stay in the city where he could pursue his musical ambitions.

One of Mark's heroes at that time was the legendary drummer, Lenny White. Never one for being backward at coming forward, Mark sat down with pen and paper and wrote to him in New York. To his utter delight, he received a letter back stating that if Mark was ever in town he should drop by. Mark thought this was too good an opportunity to miss. In order to pay his way across the Atlantic, in the summer he joined the Pete Cotton Sound playing at a Warners holiday camp at Puckpool. Pete would tell Mark not to visit London as it was full of great musicians. 'He used to put the fear of God up me,' says Mark. Taking holiday leave from his milk round between 10 and 27 September, he set off with his girlfriend from Albany, Kay Bird – who had relations in America – to fulfil his dream. Knock, knock. 'Hello. Do you remember me? I wrote to you,' he told a startled Lenny White, who was playing with the band Return To Forever. The penny dropped when Mark explained that he was the lad from the Isle of Wight.

Lenny replied: 'Why don't you come back tomorrow and show me how you can play the drums. They're in the basement.' But the following day Mark was a disappointed fellow. A flood in the house meant that Mark couldn't show off his prowess. Then again, he was also somewhat relieved, having felt genuinely apprehensive about playing in front of his hero. But Mark came away with some sound advice: 'Remember, every man must make his own chances.' It was something that Lenny had written to Mark in his original letter, and was imprinted in his memory.

On his return to the Isle of Wight, Mark resumed his milk rounds, this time living out his fantasy as a Clint Eastwood lookalike. He brought back from America a large Stetson, cowboy boots and a replica gun and holster, and would ride the range in his Bedford van.

Up to this time, Mark had also been a serious fan of guitarist John McLaughlin, so much so that he even started dressing like him on occasions. He would buy white cricket clothes from a shop in Newport high street. 'I even tried to have my hair cut like John's, and went through a very bohemian phase. The reason *he* dressed like that was because of his religious beliefs, which I didn't care about.' Mark would still go to discos and try and tell his friends there was 'a better way', dressed all in white under his duffel coat with its horned toggles. The coat had a hood attached which as far as Mark was concerned made him appear like a monk. It all added to the illusion.

Chapter Four
The fortune hunter

'I've got to go, or it's all going to go wrong,' Mark told his parents in March 1978.

'I think he had to get out because all the old ladies were smothering him with coffee and cakes. He couldn't do his job, really,' recalls Ray. Mark bought the blue Bedford van he had used for delivering milk, registration number LUR 908H, off Joe Butcher. With no knowledge of the mainland, the family were particularly concerned about London and the muggings that occurred. As a precaution against this and the possibility of theft, Ray helped his son erect a curtain rail – complete with pelmets – inside the van. They also laid a foam mattress in the back for Mark to sleep on in case his sister couldn't put him up upon his arrival in the big city. 'We made it like a little caravan. We put curtains around the back window and installed a partition behind the back of the seat,' recalls Ray.

As Mark set out on his great adventure with his drums and his Fender guitar in the back, the snow began to fall heavily. Ray told him: ' "If things don't work out, get yourself back home. If your money has gone, phone home and I'll send you some. Don't stay there." That decided him when he was going through very rough periods, when he had to put cold water on his cornflakes because he couldn't afford the milk. He said he remembered my words but he would not admit that things were going wrong. No way would he come back and say it didn't work. It drove him on.'

'When I look back, I think we must have been mad to let him go,' admits Bridget.

Arriving in London, Mark found himself being continually moved on by the police before he eventually parked up at Holloway. His sister, new to her job, was nervous of getting into trouble through his presence, either because of him parking there or staying at her flat. Says Mark: 'She didn't want to put me up, which was fair enough on reflection. If she had done, I would probably have sprawled about and not been inspired to do anything. After three nights of being bitterly cold in the van I said to Belinda that if I stayed in the van one more night I would freeze to death. If she let me stay on the floor of the flat, I promised I would get a job. I went out and found one the next day. I walked around all the music stores and was really taken by Sounds and Rose Morris, but the people who worked there were too smart and too cool. I looked a mess by comparison. I then went to Macaris at 122 Charing Cross Road and met the manager, Martin Daley. We hit it off straight away. He asked me what I could do, and I saw there were no drums around. I lied and said I was a great bass player and really handy at building things. I said I would do anything if he would just give me a job.' His new-found employment as a demonstrator and steady income provided Mark with the opportunity to move into his first London flat, at 3 Cornwall Mansions, Blythe Road, Hammersmith, west London. It was a flat-sharing block, and Mark found himself in the company of several Italians and a Colombian.

Because of Mark's exceptional percussive mind, he was able to combine his lead guitar skills with the thumb slapping technique to create the *rhythmic style* on bass for which he is today renowned the world over. With no teacher to guide him, Mark avoided the bass player's popular finger-style technique and standard walking bass-lines.

Martin was particularly musical, and he and Mark would make tapes together which Mark would take home to play to his parents. At one stage he told them that he was forming a group called Axiom with Martin and another friend but it never came to anything.

Ray recalls: 'I think at one stage Mark sensed that I didn't think he was making the progress that he should be, working in a music shop, and he told Martin to tell me that he was doing all right. Martin said, "Take it from me, one day he's going to be world famous".'

'He also said it to me in the kitchen and I was quite embarrassed,' admits Bridget.

Mark soon became friends with a guitarist called Bill Liesegang, who worked in another unit in Charing Cross Road run by Larry Macari called The Vox Shop. In September 1978, Bill received a call from Vienna stating that a singer, guitarist and drummer were required for a new group. Mark told Bill he was a great drummer and was up for the slot. Mark, naturally, was brimming over with excitement. At last he was going to be on the road with a group. He packed up his pride and joy, the silver Premier drum kit, from Blythe Road, along with his clothes and his record collection, and off he went with Bill and a singer in tow. It was freezing on their arrival at Doblergasse, 2/26a, 7 District, where they were to squat for the coming weeks. It turned out to be an absolute disaster as none of the bookings materialized. Mark spent a couple of months in Vienna with no money and no way of getting a job or social security benefit. Thoroughly disillusioned, he returned to England minus his drum kit, the other musicians having promised to send it on at a later date. It never arrived. Mark wrote various letters requesting both the kit and the money that was due to him, but to no avail. In the April he turned to Ray for help. He pleaded: 'Could you let me have the money so that I can go to Austria? I'm going to have to go out there because otherwise I'm going to lose this drum kit.' True to form, Ray handed over the cash.

Mark was later to return to Vienna and to where one of the members of the ill-fated group whom he had recently left owned a shop. Upon his arrival, what should he see in the window but his Premier kit – for sale! A cymbal had already gone. It was too much for Mark. Being a physical type, he stormed into the shop and put the frighteners on, leaving with his kit which he lugged back to England.

On his return to England, Mark, penniless, had gone cap in hand to Martin Daley seeking re-employment. There were no vacancies in the shop but, fortuitously, the owner, Larry Macari, who knew of Mark's recent trip to Austria, was present at the time. He told Mark that his bass playing had been improving steadily and did he fancy being employed as a demonstrator for Coloursound pedals, which he owned. Effects pedals are popular with guitarists, as they create different sounds (such as chorus, phase and flange). The position also came with a car – a Morris Marina 1.8 [which was later exchanged for a Mini Estate]. Mark jumped at the chance. From nothing, he suddenly had a job, a car, a suitcase full of pedals and his bass and electric guitars. It was indeed a fortunate situation to be in, if not for Larry Macari, because his new employee, far from being out selling his wares, preferred to sit in his flat all day long and play music. 'I hardly went anywhere in the whole of the six months that I was a demonstrator. In fact I went to only two shops,' admits Mark. Every Friday he was expected to make a report to Larry Macari. He would tell his employer: 'Do you know what it's like out there on the street?' Larry would sympathize, telling Mark to keep at it and not get depressed. He didn't, and was happily able to drive home to the Isle of Wight that Christmas.

By the New Year, Mark was growing restless again. He wanted to broaden his horizons and believed that America would offer greater scope for his career and talent. Larry Macari saw an opening for his Coloursound Pedals in the US market and suggested that Mark don his salesman's hat once there. Bridget's mother, Margaret, had left each of her grandchildren £500, and Mark's money had been put into a building society account. He was desperately anxious to spend it and such a sum would be ideal for his air fare. Ray had to write various letters to the American authorities stating that he would cover his son if he ran out of money. Mark was full of hope for the future. He had a travelling companion in his friend from the Island, guitarist Boon Gould. As it transpired, things went downhill all the way.

Chapter Five
Goulden days

Rowland and Joy Gould are both writers. Rowland worked for a time as a freelance journalist and broadcaster for NBC. His wife was a film critic. By 1955 they had three children, John, Paul and Gillian. Their third son, Rowland Charles, was born on 4 March in Shanklin, Isle of Wight. It wasn't long before the family was on the move again and their fifth child, Philip Gabriel, was born in Hong Kong on 28 February 1957. Joy was concerned about raising her children abroad, preferring them to have an English education. Separating from her husband, she returned with them to the United Kingdom within six months of Philip's birth. After a brief spell in Blackpool, they moved to the Isle of Wight and stayed at the children's grandfather's estate at St Lawrence. There had once been a magnificent Hall in the grounds, with a sweeping staircase, chandeliers and marble floors. It also boasted Lord Jellicoe's fireplace. The first Earl Jellicoe, born in Southampton in 1859 and created an Earl in 1925, was appointed Commander-in-Chief of the Grand Fleet at the outbreak of the First World War. Sadly, the Hall burnt to the ground in mysterious circumstances. As a consequence, the Goulds stayed in an old concrete building which was normally reserved for chickens. The family soon settled into the battery house.

Rowland Charles had been an exceptionally good baby, so much so that one of his uncles commented to Joy that he was a real boon to the family. The nickname 'Boon' was born, and has stayed with him since. Boon has some vivid memories of those early years. One of his earliest recollections is of charging out of a door and tumbling headfirst into a bed of stinging nettles. When he was two he fell off a swing and split his head open. 'That explains a lot,' he would later quip.

The Gould family arrived in Shanklin during a beautiful, hot summer. That didn't stop the children going down with mumps and measles. Boon fell over and cut his knee while playing with his favourite truck; the children had water fights and set up bonfires and played jungles in the long grass, which grew tall and tinder-dry under the glare of the sun. According to Boon, rather than cut the grass, his grandfather thought it would be quicker and easier to set fire to it. It quickly got out of control but as there was nothing else to burn down, it didn't really matter. Boon and Philip remember their grandfather, Percy Scott-Jackson, as being something of an eccentric. He would swing his two cats, Ginger and Blackie, around his head by their tails and make them talk to him by putting one under each arm and playing them like bellows! Oddly enough, the cats lived to a ripe old age. If grandmother caught the children climbing trees she would rage: 'If you fall out of that tree and kill yourself, I'll give you a damned good hiding.'

Despite the break-up of their parents' marriage, and no father around, the children had a happy childhood, although Phil suffered more emotionally than the others.

He would mostly play with Boon and Gillian. The boys had Action Man. She had Cindy. They would play on the cliffs, and even chase the fairies in the woods.

Although there wasn't much money coming through the door, the children never went without. Joy saw to that. Christmas was always an extravagant affair. The children had full stomachs and new clothes to wear. 'We never missed our father, although we knew who he was and where he was. My mother came from a large family, with six brothers, so there were always men around,' recalls Boon. 'They were all doing well in their various occupations, so we grew up with the impression of wealth although we were not actually wealthy. The best thing was growing up on the Island. It was a fabulous place for a child to grow up. We spent all our summers by the sea. The countryside was five minutes in any direction. And being a holiday resort, there were many special attractions for the tourists, which we would visit religiously every year.' The family never went on holiday apart from once to Cheddar Gorge, Somerset. It was a good job, really, because Boon suffered from car sickness.

Joy moved the family to a large house in Shanklin, where the door was forever open to visitors. She would rent a couple of rooms out to people who came to the Island in the summer to work. Boon remembers that for some reason, they were often Spanish. They unwittingly became the children's first audience. Seated in the lounge, the kids would mime to records. Boon played broom handle, Phil the buckets and Gillian would sing through a milk bottle. 'They must have been so embarrassed on our behalf,' says Boon. 'Our imaginations were fuelled by mum's fantasy view of the world. We were protected from the harsh realities of life by her belief that something good would always happen.'

As brothers, Phil and Boon got on famously, apart from the odd quarrel. Boon was a chubby and placid child. Phil was like a beanpole. Now and again Phil would annoy him so much that Boon would chuck him down the stairs. 'I was much bigger than him so I'm not proud of what I did, but it happened. We have a much better understanding of one another now.'

The terrible trio of Gillian, Phil and Boon also had their idiosyncracies. Gillian sucked her thumb. Boon bit the back of his hand, and Phil had a nervous habit of twiddling his hair. Sometimes he would twiddle so much that he would get a small bald patch on the crown of his head. Joy would plant a kiss there when he left for school, and the poor child had to endure the ribbing from his school chums through having lipstick on his head. Phil, Boon and Gillian attended St Wilfrid's, a Catholic primary school in Ventnor, six miles from their home. With his travel sickness, it wasn't a journey Boon relished every day.

The nuns, the Sisters of Mercy, but better known by the kids as the 'Penguins', ran a very strict school. According to Boon, they had a prize collection of bamboo canes, steel-tipped rulers and thick leather belts that hung down from their waists. The headmistress was called Mother Patrick. Out would come the bamboo cane if you were caught talking in the dinner hall. The sneaks were the prefects, all girls. If they saw someone open their mouth for anything but food, the culprit would receive a tap on the shoulder and it would be off down the corridor for six of the best. If ever Boon was caught, the cunning lad would make for the boys' toilet and hang around inside until the prefects gave up waiting for him to re-emerge.

Sometimes even doing a good deed got you the cane. Boon recalls: 'I remember one day when Phil wasn't feeling too well. You were not allowed to leave the table until you had finished all your food, and the mashed potato was particularly lumpy that day. Being his older brother, I thought they wouldn't mind if I offered some words of encouragement. At the end of the meal I got carted off again.' They started taking packed lunches after that.

Boon also remembers receiving the cane for not being able to complete his four times table correctly. He usually took his punishment in his stride. Phil, on the other hand, had trouble accepting the beatings. On one occasion after being caned he stormed off the school bus and went into the local police station to report the nuns for assault and battery. Gillian and Boon dragged him out. The police accepted this, because Phil's face was well known by them. He would often pack his bags and leave home. Joy would let him reach the end of the road before phoning the station and asking them to pick him up. She hoped the experience might teach him to think twice in the future. He never did.

The boys took up music at the school, but with little success. When he was seven, Phil attempted piano lessons but got put off every time he had his knuckles rapped for playing a wrong note. At the age of eleven he tried the trumpet, but that only lasted six months. Boon had a go at the recorder and the violin, but the screeching proved too much for his ears. For some reason unbeknown to him, Boon was chosen for the school choir. It was an odd choice, considering he couldn't sing. He recalls: 'After winning an inter-school singing contest one of the judges congratulated me on my excellent pronunciation of the words. I didn't have the heart to tell him I had been miming. They kept putting me in the choir, so I kept miming.'

Despite their dislike for all things at St Wilfrid's, the school boasted the highest pass rate for the 11-plus exams on the Island. Boon passed and Phil failed.

Boon was most put out when his mother bought Phil a better present after the exam – even though he had failed. The boys went their separate ways. Phil started his new term at Fairway Secondary Modern after Boon had started at the Sandown Grammar. 'He was a Fairway Flea and I was a Grammar Grub,' says Boon.

'We would slag each other off at regular intervals. He was an ignorant git and I was a snotty-nosed swot. I guess he felt a bit inferior because of his lack of achievement but he made up for it later on. I would have my nose buried in Tolkien and other fantasy books whilst he would be reading Koestler, Hesse and Castaneda. He became a regular intellectual.' Phil would somewhat grandly often sign his name, P.hilip.

In his third year, Boon had to make a choice between music and metalwork. The latter won. Phil in the meantime picked up the guitar but as quickly put it down again. He was hopeless. Joy paid for them both to have private piano tuition, but that also proved a waste of time and money. There was only one piano available, so they would invariably squabble over who was going to practise first. The result usually was that neither of them did anything. The thought of having to spend an hour playing scales was unbearable.

Phil was becoming enthusiastic about the drums, and would lay into the dining-room table at meal times. Boon then received a clarinet as a Christmas present, having suggested to his mother that he fancied taking up the instrument. He was taken aback when Joy actually produced it because he felt she couldn't afford to buy it. The least he could do was learn to play. To his surprise, he found that he enjoyed the instrument.

Their brother Paul was away at college studying the sciences during this period, and it seemed logical to Boon to follow in his footsteps. Paul was six years older than his two brothers, and it was through him that his younger brothers were introduced to the sounds of the Sixties. Boon remembers hearing the Beatles' *Sergeant Pepper's Lonely Hearts Club Band* and the *White Album.* 'It seemed to me then that to go to college and study physics and maths and listen to the Beatles was definitely the thing to do. The Beach Boys and the Rolling Stones were constantly on the turntable. I also remember the album *Disraeli Gears* by Cream – more for the psychedelic cover than the music.

'Paul had messed around with guitar at college and bought all the Beatles' song books. When I started playing guitar I went through them and found that I knew how almost every song went. And there were a lot of them.'

Brother John had joined the RAF after leaving boarding school so his younger brothers didn't see too much of him in their formative years. John dabbled in music while stationed abroad, running dances and playing bass in a small group. He bought himself out of the Forces in 1968 and returned to the Isle of Wight. After work, he would take on his evening role as a disc jockey. Says Boon: 'He was the archetypal DJ with shirt unbuttoned to the waist and long sideburns, doing impressions of Howlin' Wolf, the black blues singer. He also wore loon pants [extremely wide-bottomed trousers as worn by sailors, fashionable in the late Sixties and early Seventies] that covered his shoes and he even had a Mexican-style [droopy] moustache at one point.

'Through John we had access to all the latest releases and, coupled with his stories about being in a band, he helped fuel the fire that was to draw Phil and me into music. When we started flirting with various instruments, he would always be there to encourage us. He introduced us to musicians on the Island who were playing at the holiday camps, and gradually the spark turned to a flame until it became an all-consuming passion. He had an old guitar lying around the house which I picked up one day and couldn't put down. I asked him if I could have it and he charged me £20! That was a lot of money in 1972 but, as it transpired, it was money well spent.'

Phil's head was also becoming full of music, and he recalls: 'School for me was a waste of time. I was good at English but nothing else. In fact I didn't enjoy school at all. I was quite shy and got picked on. I didn't really establish myself until my second year. With a lot of people, if they have success as a musician, an author or in the athletics field, they gain strength from that and it justifies them as a human being. They feel like somebody. I could never accept the fact that I used to come top in English because I did it subconsciously. It was not like a source of pride where I had had to work for it. In fact a lot of things during my childhood were not quite right but when I look back I would not want to change anything because of the freedom we had. Everything was free and easy. We had a good time. There was no pressure to be "somebody" in the family. In our teens rock and roll was still something new. Music was exploding in different directions. There were a lot of stimuli and energy around.'

Boon took A Level Technical Drawing and scraped through. He did not fare so well in Maths, walking out half-way through because he could not answer the questions. He never bothered to take Physics. Music had complete control of his psyche. All he wanted to concentrate on was the guitar. All Phil wanted to play was the drums. In 1972 they formed their first group with a friend called Nigel Longhurst on keyboards and created Greyflood, playing folk-rock numbers. They sent a tape of their music to Radio One DJ John Peel, with no success. Brother John stepped in and got them their first professional booking, at the Eastcliff Club, Shanklin, where he was working. The music was alien to the disco scene but the trio did their best to win the audience over and as a result of their valiant efforts they received polite applause.

By the summer of 1973 Phil had left school and was working on the beach renting out deckchairs. It was an aimless period in his life. He had no real ambitions, like his brother Boon, who spent most of his time hanging around Shanklin. Boon's more studious friends had moved on to university. He played bass in a shambolic set-up, earning £3 a night, which was sufficient to keep him in beer money as it was only about 10p a pint then. Phil was buying records by Genesis, Gentle Giant and Yes. Boon remembers getting high on drugs one night listening to the album *Paranoid* by Black Sabbath, and going out the next day to buy it. Late in 1973 Boon joined Transmetrix in Shanklin, an electronics firm which had been owned by his uncle. He then joined his uncle's firm

Teknicron, in Wroxhall, before Transmetrix was bought back into the family. Boon did odd jobs, working on the machine line and managing the machine shops.

By the following year, Phil had started to hang around with the hippies who had stayed on the Island after the run of popular open-air festivals that had brought such major talents as Bob Dylan and Jimi Hendrix to the local populace. It was a crazy summer. Phil had been indoctrinated into their ways of smoking grass and drinking tequila. 'We used to buy a bottle, take half of the tequila out, fill up with orange juice and get drunk. We would jam all night, making a hell of a row. That's how I learnt to play the drums.' The police would often call round to sort out the din, see all the equipment and suggest that the next time they called round they would bring their own instruments and join in.

John Gould had by then left for London where he worked for various publishing and record companies, leaving his two youngest brothers to get their acts together.

In 1974 a confident Phil placed an advertisement in the local newspaper, the *County Press*, stating: 'Fantastic young drummer seeks band.' He received replies from guitarist John Wheeler, singer Mike Jolliffe and another singer, Chris Mew. Mike decided to back out. Boon stepped in on bass guitar and another musician named Rod Nicholls came in on keyboards. They christened the band Joe Bear. Their first booking was as support to a group called Bees Make Honey, at Shanklin Town Hall. It was the same location that was used in the film *That'll Be The Day*, starring David Essex. About fifty people turned up. Rod didn't last long, and Nigel Longhurst took over the keyboards role.

They picked up a residency at the Blue Lagoon on Cowes front, playing Monday, Tuesday and Wednesday evenings. They would then switch their allegiance to the Oasis in Ryde, a club they ran on Friday nights. They were playing cover versions of the Doobie Brothers and Steely Dan, and penning their own songs. Phil wrote his first song for public consumption, a teenage angst song called 'Who's the Fool?'. It went:

When I was 15 they thought I was a fool
But now I'm 17 I'm uncool.

Another song was entitled 'Love Is a Four-Letter Word'. Most of them were drug-induced. Phil was really spaced out on music – as well as other things.

The band would charge people 30p at the door on those Friday nights and 600 would pack in like sardines. Joe Bear would play on alternate Fridays, hiring in other bands in between, paying them £30. Joe Bear were certainly not out of pocket. It was a nice little earner, as the saying goes.

They also played at La Babalu club in Ryde, a large venue, holding approximately 1,000 people, and it was here in 1977 that Boon was to see his favourite at that time, Billy Idol, singing with Generation X. 'It wasn't until 1977 that I thought my demeanour might be a bit behind the times. [He had been into wearing loon pants and wearing his hair exceptionally long.] When I saw Generation X, I stood at the back feeling decidedly out of date as hordes of London types who had come down with the band cavorted at the front. Billy was begging them *not* to spit at him. Despite what I had read about punk, I thought the band were very good. I had my hair cut in 1978.'

Phil did no such thing. With his clear blue drum kit, blond hair cascading or plaited down to his waist, huge flared, patchwork denims, cheesecloth shirt, dark blue sunglasses and clogs, he was the bee's knees. But playing in clogs? 'That's probably why I've got such a good bass drum technique,' he says today. 'My timing was always slightly behind the beat, whereas Mark [King] was just ahead, on top of it. It suited me.'

During the summer of 1975, at the suggestion of John Wheeler, a certain Mark King – this 'fantastic drummer' from the other side of the Island – was invited over to play a session with Joe Bear. It was thought a good idea that Mark and Phil should have a drum battle. 'We thought it would be fun to have two drummers in the band trying to outdo each other,' remembers Boon.

'He was totally ridiculous. Manic. He blew me away. I couldn't believe it,' recalls Phil. 'He was an aggressive tyke.' Despite Phil's come-uppance, they got on famously. As the holidaymakers drifted from the Island, so too Joe Bear petered out, although John was to re-form it the following year under the name XJB with Mark, and Boon on saxophone.

Boon had met up with a girl named Sue James. They spent the summer together before splitting up. Four months later Sue appeared on Boon's doorstep declaring that she was pregnant. Boon wasn't too shocked. They married and Chani was born at 3.50 p.m. on Saturday, 4 September 1976. Not even the arrival of their lovely daughter could keep Boon and Sue together, though, and once again they drifted apart.

Phil and Mark continued their friendship, and early in 1976 Mark would turn up in his Ford Escort at Phil's home, where they would listen to the latest sounds.

Phil drifted off to play the holiday camp circuit churning out swinging little quicksteps, 'Mack the Knife'-type numbers, much to his chagrin. He knew it was the worst thing he could do musically, but then there were not that many opportunities coming his way at the time. 'I was playing the most shitty kind of music with the most awful musicians. It probably did me a lot of harm. That's probably why I'm so retarded musically and still learning today. I had to do it to earn some money.'

At the beginning of 1977, Phil, Boon, Mark and singer Mike Jolliffe got together for a Save The Whale concert at Ryde Town Hall. Mike was singing, Phil was behind the drums, and Boon and Mark alternated on bass and lead guitar. The Hall was packed when they took to the stage. Other artists had been content to play their folk numbers, and had gone down well with the audience. The latter were certainly not prepared for what happened next. From the speakers blew this weird, punk-funk music. Jazz-fusion was how they interpreted it. Whatever it was, the quartet managed to stun the audience into silence. The senior citizens at the front couldn't believe their eyes – or their ears. The fact that they didn't understand any of it signalled total victory to Mark, even if Boon left the stage thoroughly depressed. Recalls Mark: 'After the concert we were so impressed with ourselves that we went downstairs at the Prince Consort club in Ryde and asked if we could go on stage and play the same two numbers that we had covered at the concert. They agreed and we were about to begin the second one when the musicians whose gear it was said, "Don't play any more, the people don't like it." Sure enough, they didn't.'

In 1977 Boon joined a band called Big Swifty, playing guitar and saxophone on jazz-rock numbers, but he didn't last and a year later headed off to London.

Walking down Shaftesbury Avenue, he thought: 'Every other person is a musician. What hope have I got?' He saw Mark, who by this time was working at Macari's. John Gould was also in London, and Boon lodged with him, but it wasn't long before he was back on the Isle of Wight trying to decide on his future. Only a week in London had proved a terrible shock to the system after the free-and-easy lifestyle he had adopted on the Island. He hung around for the summer, playing cover numbers with a local band, picking up his dole money and lying in the sun.

By 20 December he had joined another group and was heading for the Middle East. According to Boon, the name of the group was 'one of those rubbishy hotel names'. They had made no plans and were totally disorganized. The vague notion was to stay three months. They ended up playing ninety bookings, four hours a night, with no breaks, and earning less than half the money they had expected. At least in the United Arab Emirates they could drink. The drawback was that a bottle of whisky cost £90 and a small can of beer £1.50. They didn't drink too much as a consequence. They were sometimes invited over to the tables occupied by sheikhs and their friends. On occasions this had homosexual overtones – a hands-on-knees affair, much to the band's horror. Boon was once chased around a market by a gay blade. He was as scared as hell and fortunately saw the group guitarist in a shop and darted in to join him.

On his return to the UK, Boon went back to London and landed a job with Our Price, a record shop in Charing Cross Road opposite Macari's. Once again he stayed with brother John. Mark suggested a trip to America. 'As usual, I said, "OK, great", without even thinking about it,' recalls Boon. Perhaps he should have thought a little harder on this occasion.

Chapter Six
American dream

DATELINE: Chicago, 28.6.79

Dear Mum, Dad, Nat, Blin, Well here we are! True to form nothing went to plan – flew TWA to New York, had trouble getting past Immigration and am now crossing the USA on Greyhound bus. Still, it's a very good way of seeing the place. Temp here in Chicago is 80 degrees and we're only a quarter of the way to the West Coast. Should arrive in San F'cisco on Sat. night. Tell all in a proper letter on arrival.

Love Mark.

The 21-cent-stamped, United States Air Mail postcard depicting 'Chicago's beautiful skyline as seen from the Adler Planetarium' dropped with a welcome sigh through the Kings' letterbox in Gurnard. All was going well with Mark and Boon's trip to America.

In fact it was surprising Mark got there at all. For some reason he had travelled on a single ticket, and Immigration had let him through. They landed in New York and disembarked in brilliant sunshine. They decided to head downtown to 42nd Street to board a Greyhound bus which would take them to California. While waiting for the 'A' train to transfer them to the bus depot, a man whipped out a saxophone and started playing some excellent tunes. He just as suddenly vanished on to a train. 'Wow, this is a happening place,' thought Boon.

They were relieved to seat themselves on the bus, but it was to be a short-lived feeling. The journey lasted three days and nights, and by the second day depression was setting in as they realised how far they were away from home. It was the 'What are we doing here?' syndrome. With the bus air-conditioning going full blast, they were freezing. Outside, it was baking. They found it impossible to get warm and the cramped seats were uncomfortable. Boon recalls: 'Although the price of the tickets was exceedingly cheap ($83 each) considering the distance we were travelling, by the time we added up all the money we had to spend in order to eat at the vastly over-priced truckstops, it became exorbitant.' Seeing what little money they had brought with them being whittled away did little to alleviate their worries.

Mark was to write home: '. . . It was a great way to see America, but as you can imagine the journey took its toll – especially as at every state line we crossed we went back another hour. So the days seemed to last forever!'

It was late evening when they finally arrived in San Francisco. With rucksacks on their backs, they trundled off, having given little thought to where they were going to stay for the night. 'It was hard to hold back the tears,' says Boon. 'Before we left, my brother John had warned us about the high price of hotels. We had just enough money to last us a week at the rates he had quoted.'

They came across the Western Hotel in Leavenworth Street, with a 'Vacancy' sign welcoming them inside. Running up the steps, they met the owner. 'A double room is 35 dollars,' he told them. '. . . a week' he added almost as an afterthought.

The room wasn't exactly what you would call home. In fact it was appalling. Paint was peeling off the walls and they were forced to share with cockroaches. Tired out and mentally brainstormed, they didn't care as they crawled wearily into their sleeping bags.

They woke late the next morning, and, with cheerier hearts went out for a stroll and to find their bearings. The first sight to greet them was a man running up the road carrying a child. He was wearing a purple dress. Still, they *were* in what was supposed to be the gay capital of the world. They found a greasy cafe where, for around a dollar, they could breakfast on sausage, eggs (done over-easy) and a stack of pancakes. They ate there every day.

'. . . Everywhere is open until it's time to open again and we've found a really cheap place to eat – Breakfast – two hot cakes and maple syrup – two eggs – three sausages – two cups of coffee for $1.30 . . .' Mark wrote home.

On one occasion a group of women were in the café. As Boon rose to fetch some more coffee, one of them who had been giving him the eye rubbed against him and said: 'Hello, sailor,' in a husky voice.

Boon was momentarily taken aback. Sitting at a nearby table was a man who commented: 'Watch it, son. The women in San Francisco have got bigger balls than the men.' Boon sensibly steered clear.

Although Mark wasn't into sightseeing, they followed the tourist trail, visiting the Golden Gate Bridge and Alcatraz by helicopter and Pier Thirty-Nine, a massive wooden construction with various attractions, including American collegiate Hamilton Riddle who carried out spectacular, death-defying dives into a tiny pool.

Boon recalls that he and Mark would hang out of the hotel window listening to the sounds of the guns blazing at night! Apparently it was mostly inter-family killings. On one occasion they were quietly tucking into special fried duck in a small Chinese restaurant, where you could eat a mountain of food for less than two dollars. A black patron, drunk as a lord, decided to try and leave without paying his bill. The owner grabbed him, starting a fight. Mark and Boon found themselves fending off chairs with one hand as they tried to continue eating with the other. Suddenly, the diner pulled out a knife. The Chinaman produced a gun. 'This is it,' thought the likely lads. Fortunately, one of the black's friends dragged him away into the night.

Mark had written home on 3 July: 'Dear Mum, Dad, Nathan, Hello! How are things at home? All well I hope. As you can see (from the first postcard) Boon and I are living it up in the San. Fran. hotels. Actually we've been so lucky, but I'll tell you later on, after an account of our journey . . .'

They didn't know the half of it.

The Western Hotel was full of backpacking Europeans, and included two New Zealanders, Craig and Bruce, with whom

Mark and Boon spent time. One night, they all decided to have a good time. George, the hotel proprietor, asked them to make sure they were quiet when they got back. 'Sure,' they lied. The first bar they visited was called Googles. The barmaid was called George. 'I don't remember too much about the second bar except that there was a pool table and I was talking to a rather nice Swedish girl,' recalls Boon. 'Everyone got drunk. Mark nicked the cue ball from the pool table. I'll always remember it bouncing down the hills of San Francisco smashing into parked cars.'

On their arrival back at the hotel, Mark suggested that on the count of three, they all scream. They did so and rushed to their rooms. An Irish friend called Bronson was caught on the hop by George. Bronson, being larger than George, duly punched him on the nose. He then proceeded to tear up the stairs, shouting to Mark and Boon: 'Oh Jesus. I just hit him. You've got to get me out of here.' Mark by this time was lying in bed, fully clothed, pretending to be asleep. George had phoned the police. Mark took Bronson round to the room where the New Zealanders were staying and hid him under the bed. Boon by this time had arrived back at the hotel with his Swedish friend. He unlocked the door to his room, but Mark was not inside. Relocking the door, he went upstairs with the young lady in tow. Mark, who didn't have his key, then went in search of Boon. It was turning into a Brian Rix-type farce.

Mark rushed around tapping on various doors trying to find Boon. When he eventually stumbled across him, Boon was rather slow in realizing what was going on. Mark didn't have time to wait for the key to the room. He ran back down to Craig and Bruce's room, which was next door to his and Boon's. Mark climbed out of the bay window, three floors above the ground, edged along a tiny ledge and entered his room just as the police arrived. Stripping to his underpants, and covered in brick dust he leapt into bed, as the banging came on the door. Pretending to yawn, Mark opened the door to face a gun pointing at his nose. 'Where's ya friend?' asked the police officer.

'Who, Boon?' replied Mark, looking innocent. The question was repeated. 'I don't know where he is,' came the reply. As the policeman went off to find and quiz Boon, Mark managed to reach Bronson and hustle him down the fire escape and out of harm's way. After the police had left, Boon returned to their room to find that Mark had locked him out. He was forced to sleep elsewhere in the hotel with his Swedish friend. The following morning, George told them to leave.

In a letter to the family postmarked Las Vegas on 20 July, Mark wrote: 'How are things? Boon and I got kicked out of our hotel last week for causing a riot! It was quite an adventure with armed police chasing us round the building at all hours – I'll tell you about it later because it's a very long story. So here we are in our nice new hotel. It's still very cheap so we can't complain . . .'

With the moral support of Craig and Bruce, Mark and Boon had roamed the streets until they came across the Adamis Hotel, only marginally more expensive than their previous resting place. After dumping their gear, they went for a walk. It all looked familiar. It was. Around the corner was the Western Hotel. They had gone round in a complete circle.

During this time, Mark had been anxiously awaiting a package from Macari's, in order to carry out some business transactions that he had been setting up, selling Coloursound pedals. He also needed the equipment in order to boost his and Boon's quickly disappearing resources. After three weeks in San Francisco they decided to head for Los Angeles and pastures new. Mark wrote home: 'By the time you get this letter I should be in Los Angeles – we leave on Friday the 20th, so if you have to contact me I will be at Boon's uncle's in Del Mar, California.

'Up to now I don't think very much of the States. It's too big and the people are so false I wonder how they are such a successful nation.'

On arriving in Los Angeles, Mark and Boon checked into the Hotel Cecil, directly across the road from the Greyhound terminal. It cost them $40 a week – no doubt because it had television laid on. As they got into the lift, a passenger asked where they were from. 'England,' they replied.

'You shouldn't come here. You'll either end up dead or in jail,' came the reply. Not a very auspicious start! Once again, they were invaded by cockroaches and spent the first night awake with the lights on trying to avoid their room-mates. The next day they met their Kiwi friends and spent the day at the beach. They also paid a visit to the home of the legendary keyboard player Chick Corea, but he wasn't home.

DATELINE: July 24th, 1979. 'Well what do you know?

Here we are in Los Angeles – it's so hot it's quite a bore! We've been to the beach at Santa Monica (that's round the corner from Malibu) and have teamed up with some New Zealand guys with whom we have hired a car. We've also been to Magic Mountain where they have the biggest roller-coasters in the world – they're terrifying and I had no choice but to scream my head off. Also we've been around Universal Studios seeing how they make the films and enjoying the amusements. Next we go to Las Vegas – Grand Canyon – Disneyland then back to San Diego, just outside of LA.

'LA is a worse city but I prefer it because of the atmosphere – it is 1,600 square miles, about twice the size of the Isle of Wight. It's absolutely huge. Nearly every day they have a smog warning in the city. Love Mark.'

They left early in the morning for Las Vegas. The heat was intense. The air-conditioning in the hire car tended to overheat the engine, so they left it off. Having the windows down didn't help, and tempers soon became frayed. They eventually reached Vegas at 9 p.m. and decided to visit a few casinos before sleeping in the car to save money. They entered the Golden Nugget – and stayed. Boon ended up losing about $50. Mark came out evens, although at one stage he was $400 up.

The next day they drove about twenty miles south to Lake Mead. It was 110 degrees in the shade. They spent the day in the sun and in the evening joined some Americans. Boon remembers one of them called Zeke the Bearhunter from Alaska. He had some dope on him, which he called *Alaskan Thunderfuck*. Apparently, it was lethal. Mark had never tried dope before and it was certainly not a favourite smoke of Boon. Mark, totally freaked out and legless, kept staggering towards the lake and Boon kept staggering after him to bring him back. They slept soundly on wooden benches under the stars. The next day they set off for the Grand Canyon.

Having called at a store to pick up four six-packs of beer, they pulled up at an observation post and took in the view. Boon stepped rather too close to the edge and lost his mirrored sunglasses. The next morning – having slept in the car again – Craig and Boon decided they would try and reach the bottom of the canyon. In T-shirts and trainers and with half a carton of orange juice, the intrepid explorers set off down a zigzagging mule track. It didn't take long for them to realize their stupidity. Boon wrapped his T-shirt around his head to keep the sun off. At the second watering hole they decided to turn back. By midday, scorched and breathless, they arrived back at the top, to be greeted by much hooting and hollering from Mark and Bruce, who had sensibly stayed where they were.

That evening they met up with some Americans who invited them to crash out at their camping ground, thereby avoiding the risk of being caught sleeping in the car by the park rangers.

The next morning they headed back for Los Angeles. Stopping by the Colorado river, they found a camping site with swimming pool and showers. To avoid paying, they sneaked in. All was hunky-dory until they were asked where they had pitched their tent. Moving on, they came across a smooth patch of grass and settled down in their sleeping bags for the night. They awoke to the sound of a strange whirring heading directly towards them. Over the brow of a hill they could just make out a golf cart, which missed them by inches. Ignoring this disturbance, they endeavoured to return to sleep only to be rudely awoken again when Mark was rapped across the shins with a stick. The police officer demanded to know what they were doing sleeping on a private golf course. They honestly, and quite sensibly, pleaded ignorance. At 3 a.m. they found themselves back in the car and on the road. Boon got behind the wheel and drove as the others went back to the land of nod. They arrived in Los Angeles at 10 a.m. and drove out to Malibu Beach. That evening they forked out for a motel room in Santa Monica, purely to catch up on their sleep.

It was time for the parting of the ways. Craig and Bruce were heading for San Diego, and Boon and Mark twenty miles north to Del Mar and Boon's uncle's home.

'Dear Dad, Mum, Nat, Blin, How are things? We are staying at present with Boon's uncle and aunt, who have a beautiful house overlooking the Pacific Ocean. The weather here is gorgeous, but nowhere near as hot as it was in Las Vegas, where it was a deadly 120 degrees F – unbelievable. We had a great time travelling around the desert, stopping to swim in the lakes dotted around. These were 87 degrees F and crystal clear.

'We had a letter from Macari's saying that the gear was on its way, which is a good job because the money is running out now. Boon's uncle came to the rescue here and is employing us as signwriters, which covers our bed and board.

'Musicaly [sic] California seems a dead loss and what musicians I have seen have been quite poor . . .

'Recently we did some work on Fairbanks Ranch – this is a huge ranch bought by Douglas Fairbanks which is now to be turned into luxury houses starting at 250,000 dollars. Apart from watching out for rattlesnakes and poisonous insects, all we did was pick oranges for ourselves! . . . Mark'

A letter from Macari's regarding the Coloursound equipment, dated 24 July, read: 'Thank you for the letter. We are arranging to send you separate colour samples and leaflets.' They never arrived.

Boon had not met his uncle Peter or his wife Bunny before, but he and Mark were welcomed with open arms. They spent three weeks with the family. Boon remembers that on one evening he, Bunny and Mark, after a somewhat heavy drinking session, decided to go down to the beach to watch the grunion run. Apparently, at certain times of the year these fish come inshore to lay their eggs. You can literally scoop them out of the water. Not finding any grunion around, a disappointed Bunny kept attempting to dive into the water, shouting: 'I know they're here somewhere.' Arm linked in arm, the three of them staggered back to the house.

Bidding his aunt and uncle a sad farewell, Boon and Mark met up with Bruce and Craig on one last occasion when they visited Sea World. They exchanged addresses, knowing that they would more than likely never see each other again. 'We had had a good time and had stored many good memories,' says Boon. As they were preparing to set off for England, Boon met a young lady called Linda. He didn't take much persuasion to stay on, and eventually spent six months with her in San Diego, doing odd jobs. Mark wrote to his father and asked to borrow the fare home. Their adventure together was over.

While in San Francisco on a recent visit, Mark went looking for a music shop to check out the guitars. The area that he found himself in slowly became familiar. There was little wonder. He was on Leavenworth Street. Upon closer inspection, he came across the Western Hotel. It was boarded up. The Chinese eating house had also gone. But the memories linger on.

On his return to England, it wasn't long before Mark was off on his travels once more – this time with some other musicians to Italy, where he had his first taste of Parma ham. If the food was good, the idea of working as a musician in Europe proved to be yet another disaster and Mark was soon back in London.

While Mark and Boon had been gallivanting across America, Phil had pulled himself together. In 1978, at the age of twenty-one he began studying classical music and percussion at the Guildhall School of Music in London, before transferring to the Royal Academy of Music. He had no ambition to become a classical musician, though, and was thoroughly disillusioned with the whole college scenario, but he was in London. That was his objective. In 1979, through his brother John who was by now working for MCA Records, he met up with Robin Scott, who had achieved success with his group M and the single 'Pop Music'. Robin invited Phil to join his session band on drums. Also involved were Gary Barnacle on saxophone, Robin's girlfriend Bridget (later to become his wife) on vocals and his brother Julian on bass guitar, and Wally Badarou, a Parisian session player on keyboards who had played on 'Pop Music'. Phil spent the summer with them recording an album at Mountain Studios in Montreux, Switzerland. In 1980 he worked at ICC Studios in Eastbourne, at which point he invited Mark King down to do some drum and bass guitar sessions. 'We had a fantastic time doing M's album *Official Secrets*. There were no pressures,' recalls Phil.

While studying at the Guildhall, Phil had made friends with a keyboard player named Mike Lindup. Level 42 was just around the corner.

Chapter Seven
Piano man

Nadia Cattouse was born in British Honduras (now Belize), It was then a peaceful colonial backwater, a self-governing British colony where nobody bothered anybody else. Located on the Yucatan Peninsula and overlooking the Caribbean, Belize, now an independent commonwealth country, is bounded by Mexico to the north, and Guatemala to the west. It is a mixture of rugged country, forty-five per sent tropical forest, and the longest barrier reef in the new world.

To the children, it was paradise. Nadia grew up with no television or local radio. Most people had a bamboo pole with a long aerial attached which picked up the sponsored programmes on the American airwaves. There was light music and drama from Maxwell House, religious music, country and western, big band and trad. jazz. Popular music was Duke Ellington and Count Basie – Lucky Strike cigarettes sponsored a hit parade with Frank Sinatra and Dinah Shore. In the church choir Nadia sang ancient and modern hymns, psalms, anthems, and she sang and danced to the local brukdonn, a king of soca, which combined African, Latin American and Caribbean rhythms. As a child Nadia used to sit at the piano and amuse her grandmother by playing and singing songs from all over the world. Patriotic songs swam through Nadia's young head. Church missionaries would make up crazy little ditties to which she would sing along. It was wonderful fun, but there was still a wide world out there beyond the reef

THE KING AND I... Mark King and Mike Lindup do their Level best to look cool
(London Features International).

Above: SOFA, SO GOOD... Mark
takes all the success sitting down
(London Features International)

Right: A PHYSICAL
PRESENCE... Mark doing an
impression of The Shadows'
famous stage walk *(London
Features International).*

Left: TOGETHERNESS... Mark,
Mike, Phil and Boon prior to the
departure of the brothers Gould
(London Features International).

Above: NEW BEGINNING… Mark and Mike with latest recruits Alan Murphy (second left) and Gary Husband *(London Features International).*

Below: ONCE UPON A TIME… Mike, Phil, Mark and Boon in the early days. Mark sports a sweatshirt depicting the sleeve of their first album with Polydor Records, 'Level 42' *(London Features International).*

Above: VESTED INTEREST... Mike and Mark pictured in November, 1987 *(London Features International)*.

Below: SHAVING GRACE... Boon Gould sports beard and guitar strap, while Mark and Mike are truly collared and Phil stays in the shade *(London Features International)*.

Above: WE'VE GOT RHYTHM… Cool-hand guitarists Mark and Boon lay down some funk *(London Features International).*

Below: COLD SHOULDER… Boon braves the weather while Mark coats himself in warmth *(London Features International).*

Above: YOUNG AT HEART… Level 42 in their first professional pose for Polydor in 1980. Also pictured is conga player Leroy Williams *(London Features International)*.

Below: ALL THE WORLD'S A STAGE… Mark pumps out the adrenalin as Level 42 go into full flight *(Polydor)*.

Above: ARE WE SETTEEING COMFORTABLY!… The new line-up which went down a storm during the 1989 tour *(Polydor)*.

Below: WAIST NOT, WANT NOT… Jean geniuses Mark and Mike with Gary Husband and Alan Murphy *(Polydor)*.

ALL TOGETHER NOW… One of the last photographs taken of the original Level 42 *(Polydor)*.

and Nadia always knew one day she would be part of it.

One day on the radio, she heard an announcement requesting volunteers for the Auxiliary Territorial Service (ATS). Without saying a word to her mother, Nadia straddled her bicycle and headed in the direction of the Drill Hall. On arrival, she found she was number thirty-one in the queue. There were only six places to be filled. Nadia was one of those chosen. At just seventeen years of age, Nadia found herself crossing the Atlantic Ocean with a shipload of American troops.

On her arrival in England, her first destination was Guildford, for early training. From there she headed for Edinburgh, where she joined the Signals Corps. Living in Warwick Avenue, she was more than a little surprised to find herself rooming with six London prostitutes. 'I thought, well, everybody's doing their bit,' says Nadia. Being particularly athletic, she was sent to Newton Abbot for training as a part-time physical training instructor before moving to a camp in Leith.

Nadia hadn't had time to think about home, what with the training, the singalongs around the Naafi piano and trudging back to her room in the snow with a bag of fish and chips. It all came back to her on one return trip to British Honduras. 'I remember returning home once with another girl. We went on a banana boat, which is a very exciting adventure in itself. We went via Trinidad and Jamaica. As we gradually entered the tropics, we couldn't bear to go to sleep. We just wanted to stay on deck all night because of the wonderful tropical atmosphere. When we got home and we were by the sea, we were both homesick for London. It was quite funny.' After being demobbed, Nadia spent time in Glasgow completing her training as a teacher before returning to British Honduras. The next time she returned to Britain was just as the Festival of Britain was ending in 1951. She has lived in England since.

On her return from British Honduras, Nadia was called into the Colonial Office in London, which was creating a welfare body to cater for new arrivals. She took charge of the women's section and the migrants' welfare. 'They were British citizens, not immigrants or aliens,' stresses Nadia. She joined the Commonwealth Drama Group, which was housed in a large building behind Harrods store in Knightsbridge. Her interest in this area of the arts gradually began to take over and she was invited to take part in a tour of Britain, which was where she was to meet her first husband, David Lindup, a composer/arranger of musical scores. They married in 1958.

Their son Michael was born in the small hours of 17 March 1959, St. Patrick's Day, at Guy's Hospital, London. If the wind was blowing in the right direction you could at one time just make out the sound of Bow bells, so baby Michael was on the fringe of being born a Cockney. 'I have this picture in my mind of when Michael was first put in my arms with his spiky hair. I sang a little lullaby that I knew. Gradually his eyes, which had been closed, lifted up and gazed at me with complete intelligence,' recalls Nadia. The family lived in Southwark for three years before moving to Wimbledon.

The Lindups had a wide taste in music. Tchaikovsky was played alongside Count Basie, Pete Seeger and Joni Mitchell. The family pet, Polly the parrot, would join in, attempting to mimic Nadia's vibrato as in 'Climb Every Mountain'. Michael's earliest recollections are of hearing music around the house. 'One of the first tunes I used to sing when I was in my playpen, when I was two years old, was 'Desafinado' by Stan Getz, which had a cool, west-coast jazz sound. Learnt it parrot-fashion from the record. Stan Getz more or less played the tune but he did his own version. There would be a few improvisations. I used to sing it and my mum started singing along and she didn't quite get it exactly right so I got very upset and was telling her that it was wrong.'

Nadia recalls: 'Rightly or wrongly, I came to the conclusion that Michael was very musical.'

Michael's sister Pepita was born when he was approaching his third birthday. As they grew up, there was quite a bit of one-upmanship and squabbling between them. Pepita was born suffering from brittle bones, which she had inherited from her father, so Nadia was often with her in hospital.

Nadia and David separated in 1964 when Michael was five, and they divorced in 1968. Nadia was heavily involved in the folk world by this time and annually attended the Edinburgh

Festival. The family would spend their summer holidays in the city and visit the Highlands, which they grew to love and still have a great affinity with to this day. Both David and Nadia were to remarry, although her relationship was not to last.

Michael visited British Honduras for the first time when he was six. It was Christmas. He remembers being given a toy boat, and sleeping under mosquito nets. Back in Wimbledon, he began piano lessons and at primary school he took up the violin. He kept at the violin for a year before his enthusiasm waned. 'I was fed up with it. I can pick up a violin now and play one tune, one of those you get in your first book of violin pieces, very badly. On the piano, the simple pieces led to the Grade 1 certificate. I changed teachers twice and got up to Grade 5 with a Mrs Todd. I was also improvising from quite an early age. My sight reading has always been poor simply because I could pick up things by ear, and this developed well. I started making up little pieces with encouragement at home. We had a piano and I bashed away trying to work out tunes I had heard and put harmonies on. It was good fun. Christmas was a very social time and we would play hymns and carols and sing round the piano.'

His parents' separation did not affect the young Michael in terms of anything being interrupted. His father would pick the children up every other weekend, and his stepfather, Bryan, came on to the scene and for a while took over the fatherly role when Michael was about ten. The family suffered some hard times, but Nadia was wonderfully strong and supportive to her children.

Michael spent six years at Holly Mount Primary School before joining Wimbledon Chase Middle School when he was eleven. He was there for two years before starting at Raynes Park High School.

Nadia had been closely monitoring her son's musical ability. It had been suggested by one of his teachers that he should try for one of the bursaries for a Saturday class at music college, but nothing transpired. On one of her frequent visits to Edinburgh, when Nadia was working with musicians Sidney Carter and Jeremy Taylor, they were invited to the 15th-century cathedral in Manchester. 'We were one of the first to be singing themes and musical exploration songs on a Sunday programme on ABC Television called *Hallelujah*,' remembers Nadia. Michael was nine years old at this time. While at the cathedral. Nadia was informed about Chetham's School of Music. It was an old building in the middle of Manchester which had been founded by Sir Humphrey Chetham in the 17th century. It was originally a school for orphans before becoming an independent school. In 1969 it became co-educational and a specialist music school. Nadia returned to Wimbledon with news of the school, but little more was said until five years later.

When he was fourteen, Michael was interviewed and subsequently offered a place at Chetham's. Nadia was completely against the idea of her son attending boarding school, but she knew how important the move would be for his musical education. It was only when Michael left home that he fully appreciated what a good relationship he had with sister Pepita. A friend of Michael's, Tim Smithers, was also starting at the school, and it was his parents who had again sowed the seeds in Nadia's mind for her son to attend.

Michael was particularly excited about starting at boarding school and being away from home, although he had no idea at the time where it would lead. His excitement soon turned to homesickness during that first term. At 6.30 a.m. the boys would be awoken. They would make their way to an old stone bathroom containing tiny sinks to wash in. More often than not it was freezing cold. Sometimes the headmaster, Mr Vickers, would wake them. He would walk round with two dogs. When the boys heard the click-click of their paws on the floor, they knew exactly who was coming to watch over them. Not only did they have to wash their faces, they had to strip off their shirts and scrub the backs of their necks and under their arms. A stickler for cleanliness, was Mr Vickers. His nickname was 'Boss'.

Two-thirds of the boys were boarders, with homes as far flung as Beirut, Switzerland and Norway. Half-term for Michael would sometimes be spent in Wales, other times in Scotland. 'Bryan and I would go up to Edinburgh in the Triumph Herald and stay there a week with mum, and then drive up the west coast of Scotland for a holiday. The idea of having a crofter's cottage in the Highlands seemed like a dream. It's still magic up there. It feels like a home from home,' says Mike now. It was understandable that Michael looked forward to his breaks. He found being in the middle of Manchester both restrictive and oppressive. 'It was very dull and grey. I didn't like Manchester at first. It's not pretty. The northern gloom came over me a bit although the people were friendly. I found it very easy to talk to them. I enjoyed our school trips to the Lake District where we would go on walks to clear our lungs. It's wild, bleak and wonderful. I loved those geography field trips. I grew up with a feeling for the countryside and nature.'

In fact Michael was very much an introvert as a child. He got heavily involved in bird watching when he was twelve and joined the Young Ornithologists' Club, the junior section of the Royal Society for the Protection of Birds. He would often cycle off on his own to Richmond Park, near Wimbledon, at weekends, with his binoculars. He never thought of himself as a loner, of getting away from things, or people. He would become engrossed in his stepfather's books on arachnids and insects. Little black things crawling around became objects of extreme interest. He was also keen on art and would design Christmas cards. Radio was much more of a constant companion in his youth than television, which the family went without for four years. It was one of the best things that could have happened at the time, as it opened the door to so many other opportunities. He would pop round to the corner shop with his pocket money and buy an Airfix model, sit in his bedroom making the model, and listen to Kenny Everett on Capital Radio on Saturday mornings. He was not partisan to any particular style of music at this time. The only record he had bought was a K-Tel compilation, *22 Dynamic Hits*. It included 'Lean on Me' by Bill Withers. 'Hold Your Head Up' by Argent, 'Brandy' by Looking Glass and 'Goodbye To Love' by the Carpenters.

At Chetham's he was introduced to the sounds of Emerson, Lake and Palmer. He was excited by this trio of chart musicians playing classical-style compositions. The inspiration led to Michael (keyboards), drummer Dave Adams and bass player Julian Gregory forming a group. They made up their own pieces. 'It was probably pretty awful,' recalls Mike. But through his friends he began to hear other records like *Dark Side of the Moon* by Pink Floyd, Stevie Wonder's *Innervisions* and Genesis. Michael was fifteen at the time. They called themselves LAG (the initial letters of their surnames). Rehearsals were carried out in the percussion room and in the music hall before the term pop concert, at which Michael would borrow a string machine. The group was very much a hit–or–miss affair and they lasted a year, appearing at two concerts for the pupils and those teachers who dared to show their faces. Having said that, they went down reasonably well. Other acts were playing either 'Stairway To Heaven' (Led Zeppelin) or singing in barber-shop style. Anything but classical was the order of the day.

At Chetham's there was an electronics wizard called Simon Walker who built his own radio station in the sixth form block. He named it Radio Valentino. Michael helped run it. They had an old Revox reel-to-reel tape recorder and would invent pieces on guitar and piano, record and broadcast them. They also made up jingles. Michael left all the electronics to his friends. The first electronic instrument he was to own was a second-hand Mini Moog.

Michael's first love at Chetham's was a girl called Josephine Wells, who was later to be known for her work with Kissing The Pink and later still as saxophone player with Tears For Fears in 1985. She also did a spell with the Communards. In fact Josephine was the girlfriend of Tim Smithers. Michael was in love from a distance. He never really dared approach her. When he eventually did, she turned him down – in the nicest possible way.

Dating took on a very public school air. Once you asked some-one out, that meant you were going out with each other, which meant that you sat together at meal times and sat with your arm around each other in the television lounge. There were numerous conventions to adhere to. Michael was young, immature and shy. A normal relationship would last no longer than a week. As a result he grew very tense, which reflected in his relationships with the opposite sex, who found it far more relaxing in his company to remain as friends. It duly became a blow to his ego and he set up barriers, making sure he would not be hurt in the future. He became his own worst enemy. It reflected in his school work at times. He would leave his homework to the last minute, then find that he couldn't complete it in time. In the fifth year, he cracked and ran away.

He boarded a train at Manchester's Victoria Station and got off at Wilmslow, Cheshire. He spotted a policeman and tried his damnedest to act normally. Michael made his way to the home of Jane Clarke, a school friend. At 5 a.m. he meekly knocked on the door. Jane's mother answered and let him in. 'She was great. She gave me a sleeping bag and the next morning gave me a lift back to school. As we arrived the headmaster was talking to a police sergeant in the yard waiting to see me. The house master, John Cleaver, saved my skin by smoothing the situation over,' recalls Mike. Tim Smithers, by now a senior prefect, asked Michael why he had not told any of his friends he was going. 'I suppose that was the most extreme point I got to of escapism. I realized I was running away from myself. It taught me the lesson that things never get better if you run away.' The school thoughtfully didn't worry Nadia about her son's abdication from his prep, and she didn't find out until Michael told her during the holidays.

Michael soldiered on at Chetham's. He felt he suffered academically, although he passed five O Levels, including CSE Grade 1 in French. He went on to take A Level Music, an increasing passion. He joined the Chamber Choir and sang tenor before switching to bass. In 1976 he travelled to Switzerland with them on a trip arranged and paid for by the boys' choir in Basle.

He left Manchester at the age of eighteen as a semi-accomplished pianist and percussionist, knowing that he wanted to seek a career in music, perhaps in an orchestra. Michael had auditioned for the Royal Academy of Music, the Royal College of Music and the Guildhall School of Music. He eventually joined the last-named in September 1977 on the graduate (teachers') course.

'I didn't think I was virtuoso enough to be a performer. By then I was taking percussion which I had started at music school at the suggestion of the old head of music, as well as piano. I had never really thought about it. You had a first and a second study, as well as composition. I was getting bored with the clarinet and wasn't practising.

'Percussion, on the other hand, was great. It was fairly easy to pick up and opened the door to orchestral playing, with timpani, side drums, cymbals, tambourine and triangle. I was involved in all orchestral playing at Chetham's, having always liked classical music. On the end-of-term speech day, originally staged at Manchester Town Hall, we had to parade through the city dressed in these old-fashioned uniforms, at which time we were jeered at by other boys. We wore long black coats with brass buttons, orange socks and shorts.' At Guildhall he quickly became involved in the pop workshops as a drummer where he got a rhythm section together with other singers. They had a big band and appeared at several concerts doing anything pop- or jazz-influenced. He thought about picking up some session work, but dismissed the idea because his sight reading was so bad.

One day while walking down the corridor during the second year of his three-year course, he heard this incredible drum playing, the like of which he had not heard before. Popping his head round the door, he saw this young man with blond hair behind the set. It was Phil Gould, who was having part-time lessons with Michael's percussion teacher, Bob Howes. They immediately struck up a friendship, and they spent many happy hours at Phil's flat in Clapham, south London, listening to the sounds of Herbie Hancock and Miles Davis. Rifling through the jazz record collection in the Guildhall's music library, Michael discovered many of the names of which Phil had spoken.

A name that didn't pop up in this collection but cropped up in conversation was that of Mark King. They met in Oxford Street in 1979. Michael had just bought some Billy Cobham drumsticks and was feeling particularly excited about trying them out. To Mark, worldly-wise after his trips to Europe and America, Michael was an unknown quantity musically. He was trying to discover whether he was 'hip'. He most certainly wasn't, although he wanted to be.

On his return from America in autumn, 1979, Mark had been re-employed by Macari's at the firm's distribution factory in Edgware. During one of his trips into central London he met up with Peter Bernini who, according to Mark's fantasy world, had the nearest sounding name to Chick Corea of anyone he had yet come across. Peter said he was in London putting together a band to take to Italy. Once again, Mark dropped in the line about being a great drummer. Peter said he had already filled that slot but that there was still a vacancy for a bass player. Mark, naturally, also said he was great at that instrument. Peter left Mark telling him that all the equipment would be sorted out. A young and impressionable Mark found himself teamed up with Peter, an Argentinian and a Brazilian, who began rehearsing cover versions of Earth, Wind And Fire numbers. The group ended up travelling to Germany to play a one-off show, before returning to Italy, where a depressed Mark spent his twenty-first birthday. Returning to England, he told Martin Daley that he was fed up and had decided to return to the Isle of Wight. Martin eventually coaxed Mark back to the mainland, telling him he could stay at his flat in Walthamstow for nothing if he helped convert it into two flats. 'I set about destroying the place,' says Mark. 'It's always easier knocking things down than it is rebuilding them.' At that time Mark was on the dole, bringing in about £13 a week.

Boon Gould had ended his relationship in America and had returned to England. In January 1980 he arrived in London with £14 to his name and no idea of what he was going to do. He stayed with friends for a few weeks, knowing he had to move on. He ended up contacting Mark, and was invited over to Martin's Walthamstow flat. On arrival, he found the place in a complete shambles, with brick dust and building materials lying everywhere. Although Martin was having the place 'done up', it remained the same all the time that Boon was there. Mark was sleeping on a small camp bed in a corner of the front room. Boon spread out his sleeping bag on the bare floorboards. It was to be his bed for the following six months.

'It was freezing that winter and there was no heating,' he remembers. 'I used to wake up in the morning with frozen knees. That summer when the weather got really damp I would get up in the morning and be unable to walk for an hour or so.'

Their only means of cooking was a small Baby Belling electric hotplate and grill. It would take them about two hours to boil three potatoes. It didn't help that they were signing on the dole at the time, so money was tight. Boon remembers Martin charging them

£5 a week each which, in the circumstances, he considered was rather steep. 'We could afford fish and chips twice a week but we usually bought meat balls in tomato sauce and egg noodles, costing 50p for two,' says Boon, who was head chef. They managed to keep their spirits high, nevertheless, helped by the fact that upstairs Martin had an eight-track studio and a small soundproofed room containing a drum kit, with a couple of amplifiers downstairs. Mark spent many hours writing and playing with Phil and Boon. Phil wasn't so hot on piano so would end up on drums most of the time. Mark and Boon would swap between the bass and lead guitar, as neither had a preference for an instrument. It was all good fun. Boon was also playing more saxophone at the time.

Some of Mark's material was to turn up on his solo album, *Influences*, released in 1984. Another bass riff was to form the basis to Level 42's hugely successful single, 'Hot Water', inspired by the fact that there was no heating in the flat.

At the time of Boon's arrival, Mark was playing with a band called Reflex, having taken over the drumsticks from Phil Gould. Leader of the band was a keyboard player called Paul Fishman, a well-respected session musician whom Mark had met in London's Trident Studios. Apparently Paul was not willing to play live until Reflex had secured the perfect management deal. As a result, they rehearsed the same seven songs, six times a night. 'These were the only people that I had met in London doing music so it was my way in,' says Mark. 'I really enjoyed Reflex and thought it was going to be terrific. We were always borrowing precious hours in equally good studios because Paul had a lot of contacts. Unfortunately, for that year I was with them, nothing happened.'

Several years later Reflex were to have a hit with 'The Politics of Dancing'. Paul had a saying: 'We can all play a million notes a minute.' He dreamt it up thanks to Mark who, when he grew bored, would thrash around the drums.

As he was settling in to the routine of doing absolutely nothing, Boon received a call out of the blue from Bill Liesegang, whom he had met briefly the previous year. Bill was looking for a bass player for his heavy metal band Xero. Boon had to audition, and was collected by the drummer in his black cab and transported to the rehearsal studios in Greenwich, south-east London. 'Playing heavy metal is an art form unto itself,' says Boon. 'It may sound simple but my fingers were raw by the time we had finished.' Boon played sufficiently well for him to join the band. The experience proved invaluable, as they did numerous gigs and recordings, and completed tracks on a couple of heavy metal compilation albums, one of which was entitled *Metal For Mutha's*, on the MCA label.

'I think Boon may have liked to be the bass player in Level 42,' says Mark. 'I certainly wouldn't have minded being the drummer. It was apparent that all this "slap and tickle" on the bass, as the boys liked to call it, was becoming one of the noteworthy things about our music. It sounded different, whereas if I played the drums it sounded the same as anybody else.'

In February 1980 Phil suggested that Mark should get together with himself and Mike Lindup for a jam in the Guildhall's rehearsal room. Phil would play drums, Mark was happy to switch to bass ('Any way to make it pay' was his motto), Mike was behind the keyboards and on guitar was Phil and Mike's friend from college, Dominic Miller. Mark ended up borrowing a bass guitar. Dominic had his own guitar, Phil used a makeshift college drumkit and Mike used a battered old upright piano and borrowed the college's 50 watt HH PA system. It was all pretty inconsequential, although they decided to get together again. 'We just borrowed some equipment and mucked about and didn't think about what kind of music we were playing or what it was called. It just was,' says Phil.

On the second occasion, Boon also showed up. Now they had two guitarists. 'I don't remember a note we played and didn't think too much about it except that it had been fun,' says Boon. 'We all went back to our own things, although we did make a date for the following week.'

Mark was still jamming with the group Axiom, who rehearsed occasionally at Martin Daley's. As the idea of Level 42 took hold, Mark opted out of Axiom, who later broke up.

Dominic failed to show at the next rehearsal ('He was actually much better than me,' admits Boon) so they were down to a four-piece. 'I think we did "Mr Pink", "88" and the backing for "Love Meeting Love" [Level 42's first single] at that time,' recalls Boon. 'Everything was instrumental and we had no other thoughts apart from just enjoying ourselves. Phil was living with [his brother] John and we started spending more time there even though it was twenty miles across London for us to get home. Therefore John was getting the low-down on the situation. I remember Mark sitting in a broken peacock chair in the living room of John's flat in Balham, stating, "I'm going to be a millionaire by the time I'm thirty." You knew by the sound of his voice and the look in his eye he wasn't going to fail. He would win all the money when we played cards. John used to get most upset.'

More and more they ran through the musical ideas being turned out by Mark and Mike. It was the latter who arranged their first booking through the entertainments secretary of the Guildhall Students' Union. They were to play in the students' bar, located in the middle of the Barbican flats complex, eight minutes' walk from the college. 'We said we wouldn't be loud because there was a broken window behind where we were playing,' says Mike.

No sooner had they started the concert than the police were on the doorstep telling them to turn the sound down as they had received complaints from the owners of the neighbouring flats. They did as they were told and turned down, although they were still reasonably loud. They had planned to play three numbers by Mark, and 'Haunted House' by Lee Oscar, who used to be the harmonica player with War. It was the only cover version the four members of the soon-to-be-born Level 42 were to play. The residents complained yet again, and the police returned to pull the plug on the beginning of the third number. 'We did a song called "Mr Pink",' recalls Phil. 'It was all really rough then but people responded to it. It was incredible they actually liked it. We had no confidence then.'

Mark and Boon had spoken about coming up with a number as the group's name for the occasion. They wanted something that would have no connections with anything until the audience had heard their music. Mark suggested 88 as it was short and could be easily remembered. Several days later Phil and Mark spotted a poster for Rocket 88, the name adopted by Jack Bruce and friends. It was too close for comfort, although '88' was later to be used as the title for a track on *The Early Tapes* album. If they were to continue together, they would have to come up with something new.

Chapter Eight
An elite beginning

Early in 1980, Andy Sojka was rehearsing a band called Atmosfear at the back of his record shop, All Ears, in Harlesden, north-west London. They eventually recorded a song called 'Dancing in Outer Space' in a small eight-track studio. At first, no major record company would touch it so Andy released it independently under his Elite Records label and it quickly became a minor disco classic. The song was licensed to MCA Records because Andy could not handle the demand. John Gould, at this time head of promotion at MCA, was the first person to contact him about Atmosfear and to suggest a follow-up. In the same breath, John mentioned that two of his brothers were playing in a band, and would he be interested in hearing them. Andy was certainly not looking for another act to sign to Elite but was prepared to give them a listen. On hearing the news, Phil Gould approached Robin Scott of M and asked if he could see his way clear to help out by paying for the hire of a rehearsal studio for a couple of days; Robin duly obliged. They found a place called Hollywood Studios in London, a complex of soundproofed rooms.

'We hired the big room because we wanted to create a good impression,' says Boon. 'When we arrived we heard the sound of high-energy funk emanating from one of the other rooms. It was a band called Light Of The World, a sort of British Earth, Wind And Fire. We started getting an inkling of what was happening in London at that time. It seemed that the current underground was for home-grown funk, similar in style at least to what we had been doing for the last few months.'

Accompanied by John Gould, Andy arrived with a completely open mind. 'I had the feeling whilst I was watching them that they were just another jazz-rock outfit in the Mahavishnu Orchestra, Herbie Hancock mould without the funk, and all those groups that used to bore me absolutely rigid,' he recalls.

'If anything, I thought they would be good session musicians. They reminded me of Friendship, an American group. I wanted to know what they had in terms of bass lines. Mark King said he had one particular riff and played it. I said, "Let's have some lyrics to that and it could be incredible." It had a Latin feel to it but was unlike anything I had heard before. Phil played along to it, Mike sort of joined in and Boon didn't know what to do.'

Says Mark: 'We always asked John Gould's advice at that time, as we had always talked about him managing us and being the fifth member of the band. I was definitely someone who was led by others and wasn't in control of anything. I played bass and guitar in front of Andy. It was just a collection of riffs. I can remember his face, because it was the first time he had seen us, being expressionless. He said that most of it was rubbish but there was the one tune he liked. We were really excited about it.'

There was some consternation as to who would do the singing and they considered bringing in an outsider to do it before it finally came down to be Mark's responsibility. The following day, Mark and Boon started writing. Mark would sing a phrase and Boon would note it down. Gradually an idea emerged. Says Boon: 'The title actually came from Mark misreading something I had written. I wrote "Love Making Love" but he read it "Love Meeting Love". Our first hit was born.'

A week later they played the finished version to Andy Sojka, who was happy to record it. First of all they had to sign a six-month recording contract with Elite Records, and deliver two singles and an album during that period. John Gould took on the managerial role. By this time the band had agreed on the name Level 42. There are several versions of how the name was conceived. Boon recalls that they had already decided to call themselves 42. He and Mark had been reading the science-fiction book, *The Hitch-hiker's Guide to the Galaxy* by Douglas Adams. In it, 42 is the answer to the question, 'What is the meaning of life?' John wasn't too struck on the name. Apparently he was sorting out some contracts with his lawyer and voiced his opinion on the subject. The lawyer suggested preceding 42 by the word Level, thus extending it. The band liked it so it stuck.

Andy Sojka says: 'I went to my solicitor about signing them up and said they were called 88. He said why not call them 42. He explained that it was from *The Hitch-hiker's Guide to the Galaxy*, so I wrote down a list of words that would fit well with 42 and Level seemed to work. I called up Mark and said, "You're now called Level 42" and he replied "I don't care what we're called as long as we make records." '

The band had already decided that they did not want to use the standard instruments associated with funk if they could possibly be avoided, which is in itself ironic as most of the equipment they used professionally for the recording was borrowed. Mark had been using a Gibson EB-2 semi-acoustic bass. The screw from one of the machine heads was missing and the cog would continually fall out. It didn't record well, and he then used an old Hayman bass that was lying around in the studio. The band was keen on using synthesizers, thus creating something unique. Mike had obviously not had experience in this field, so Phil suggested that he phone Wally Badarou, whom he had met the previous year in M.

Originating from West Africa, Wally grew up in a mixed musical culture and began his career as a keyboards session player in Paris. Having previously worked with Phil and Mark, he was more than happy to be involved in the making of the single and the band dug deep into their meagre reserves to cover the cost of his flight to London. At the time, Wally was signed to a French record label and was therefore in no position to join Level 42 on an official basis, although the subject had been broached. But since that time, he has always been known as the band's fifth arm. He has always enjoyed working relationships with other keyboard players although he senses that during the recording of 'Love Meeting Love' Mike Lindup was probably slightly nervous of his presence and it took a little while for the two of them to get to know and understand one another. There was never any question of jockeying for seniority. There were no rules or guidelines to adhere to as the mutual respect was self-evident from the outset.

Wally was particularly struck by Mark's bass technique. He recalls: 'When I first met the band I thought Mark was overwhelmingly brilliant – and he still is. He was playing the kind of music that I have always been into. Having said that, I never thought Level 42 could make a living out of that music and was really surprised that we achieved what we did. It is a combination, not only of Mark's bass playing but also the ideas behind it.'

They recorded the song in the 16-track Gateway Studios in Clapham, south London, in March 1980. Wally added a clarinet part to the second verse, Mike arranged a piano intro which, as far as Andy was concerned, made the song, and Dave Chambers augmented on saxophone. The recording went off quickly. It was a good job, as Andy didn't have much money to play with, so they couldn't afford to waste valuable time. Says Boon: 'Wally's synth playing was magical. He was doing things with the instrument no one had ever dreamed of. He was a very influential player. Mike did all the acoustic piano work and watched Wally like a hawk in order to understand this new-fangled electronic wizardry.' Being so much in Wally's shadow can't have been easy for Mike, although he was content for the session player to take a leading role. Mike was there through his own obvious talent, and his efforts have made him an integral part of the band. Mike had to hire in keyboards as he had no gear of his own for the occasion.

Andy recalls: 'Boon was so reticent about the whole thing, I didn't even know he had written the lyrics. I thought Mark was the sole composer on the record because nobody told me otherwise. In fact it was only after we had made the record and released it that Boon said, "Oh, I wrote the lyrics".'

Three thousand copies of 'Love Meeting Love'/'Instrumental Love' were released to the British public on the Elite Records label in April 1980. 'It was all really rough,' recalls Phil. 'Everybody wanted to hear a bad recording; it was supposed to be "street cred" and all about energy, not finesse.'

Andy Sojka waited to see which major record company would leap to the task of distribution. John's contacts stood the single in good stead and it received plenty of air play, including Powerplay on Radio Luxembourg. Polydor Records picked up on it and almost immediately re-released it. By August it had peaked at number 61 in the singles chart. On 6 September 1980, the number 1 single was 'Start' by the Jam, followed by 'Ashes to Ashes' (David Bowie) and '9–5' (Sheena Easton). The review in *Blues & Soul* magazine read: 'Level 42 are a new band from the same Harlesden stable that produced Atmosfear and Stop, and "Love Meeting Love" is quite simply not only the most ambitious project of this kind to date but also the best. Both sides stand out in their own right with the musicianship surpassing all their previous attempts . . . instrumentally it's as tight as a drum with full credit to the bassist for his fluent foundation and keyboard player for a really neat synthesizer solo.'

The Level 42 buzz had started, with many unsuspecting fans presuming that the band were black because of the sound. In London there were a group of disc jockeys calling themselves Funkmania, they loved the record and played it continuously in the clubs. This was to prove more of a launching pad for the band than radio plays. 'They took us under their wing as a genuine Brit-funk band,' says Boon.

'I remember spending holidays on the west coast of Ireland, and in cottages in north Wales, and Luxembourg was the radio station we used to listen to at night,' says Mike. 'Suddenly, to actually hear something that I was on being Powerplayed on Luxembourg was almost more than words could portray. I also vividly remember Peter Powell playing it on Radio One. We never thought of ourselves as being a jazz-funk band. We just played how we wanted to play. Obviously our playing was influenced by the musicians we liked – Miles Davis, John McLaughlin, Mahavishnu Orchestra, Herbie Hancock, Chick Corea, Jimi Hendrix, Cream. Also with three of us being drummers, our rhythmic, percussive playing was a kind of funk. It was just like the beginning of something that could be really good. Andy Sojka saw a gap in the market for what we were doing as part of the new British jazz-funk scene. It was this market that took us under its wing.'

In fact at one stage, Andy was in a panic. 'A lot of people said Mark was a great bass player but the rest of it wouldn't happen in a black market, and I panicked. I thought that if it didn't work in a black market, I wouldn't know how to do anything with it. One day, completely out of the blue when we thought it had peaked and finished in the dance charts, I got a call from Polydor saying they would like to sign the single up and how much did I want? The Level 42 single had cost about £1,500 to make and that was an awful lot of money for me then. I said "£5,000". Polydor said no and I said "bye-bye". They called back with a licensing deal, offering £8,000 over two singles.'

Because of their new-found success, the band had to make personal appearances. At Brent Fair, DJ Robbie Vincent gave Mike and Phil a big build-up. Mike was extraordinarily embarrassed about going on stage to talk about the song. No wonder. He remembers wearing an 'awful' brown shirt with rounded collar and a Marks & Spencer jumper. 'We were very unhip looking blokes.'

Level 42 spent June and July writing and rehearsing new material. They spent some time working in the Gould household's garage on the Isle of Wight. It was very cramped and they sounded awful. Mike had left the Guildhall in July and was living at home with his mother in Wimbledon. Boon had left Xero and was crashing with Mark at John's two-bedroomed flat at 57 Rowfant Road, Balham, London SW17, having left Walthamstow.

Andy was concerned about getting an album out of the band before his six-month contract with them expired. He asked the band if they had any new material and they said loads. 'I went along to a rehearsal in Victoria where they were due to show-case me the songs to go on the album. All I got was a rehash of the very first tape I had heard back in March. I was not happy. I told them it was all very well but I knew the stuff inside out. They said it was all they had. It was not on. I had signed them to a major label; they were a bunch of good musicians, not brilliant but good; they had a deal and they were kicking me in the teeth. I spoke to John Gould about it. He replied that if they said that's all they had, then that was all they had.

'I thought I had better make the most of what amounted to a bad job. I was after eight or nine songs. They had got a lovely instrumental called "Woman", and the songs "Wings of Love", "Autumn" and "Love Meeting Love". The rest were jazz-rock instrumentals.'

In August they were given ten days in Hillside Studios, Streatham, to record the album. 'I was excited about the prospect of the group being offered a deal, and making a record,' says Mike. But working from 10 a.m. to 6 p.m. every day, it was a trying time, with them not knowing much about studio techniques, or what they were doing musically and where, if anywhere, they were heading.

It didn't help when, returning from lunch one day, they overheard the engineer comment: 'Why don't you get some session musicians to do this, it'll be much quicker. These guys are crap.' They were mortally offended.

'If you're going to make an impression, you have to shout about yourself. Listening back to it now, it sounds very rough and ready, which it was. But we were a group, and we were very proud of that fact,' says Mike.

On the stroke of 6 o'clock, they would rush to the nearby park to play football and release their pent-up energy.

Wally Badarou again played on keyboards and proved an inspiration. 'With everything they had that was remotely rock-orientated I would sit with Mark or Wally and we would try to make it blacker,' says Andy. 'He really inspired them to play better and probably to behave themselves because they may well have gone off into long, rambling guitar solos had we not put a stop to it. They do not help sell a black record.' Andy felt that Boon was struggling to fit in with his sound, but was loath to change his guitar or technique. 'People were expecting a certain type of guitar playing. I had an idea of what was expected. It was simply a question of finding the right balance,' says Boon.

The band left Hillside with the album incomplete. With little money to speak of and even fewer bookings to look forward to, Boon started doing odd jobs through the Manpower temping agency. After sweeping the odd road and earning less than £50 a week he met up with the foreman of a warehouse which dealt in heavy oriental carpets. He signed off at Manpower and took on a full-time role. He desperately needed ready cash as Sue had been in touch explaining that she wanted to send their daughter Chani to private school. He ended up working seven days a week, ten hours a day. He remembers a seventeen-year-old youth working alongside him who was into jazz-funk and who would travel around the country listening to bands. When Boon told him he played with Level 42, the funkster 'freaked out'. Boon even roped in the rest of the band into jobs at the warehouse so that they could earn some pocket money. Doing odd jobs was nothing new to Mike Lindup, who had previously earned extra money clearing tables at London's Royal Festival Hall and working as a kitchen porter.

Their lucky break came when ATV Publishing signed them and gave them a £5,000 advance. The welcome money was poured into equipment. Mike bought a second-hand Fender Rhodes and a second-hand Mini Moog; Mark bought his first Jay Dee bass and a Trace Elliot amplifier. He had originally thought of purchasing a Fender Precision or WAL, but the price tags ruled that idea out. Then he set eyes on the Jay Dee in Sounds music shop in London's Shaftesbury Avenue and he knew he had to have one. He was struck by the fact that it looked somewhat like an Alembic, his dream bass, and was knocked out by the sound with its active circuitry. The Jay Dee was £700, including the case. Mark couldn't afford it but as the bass was on 'sale or return' from its maker, John Diggins, he phoned up and they struck a deal.

'With this instrument my playing is going to go sky high,' he said at the time. The sales of the Jay Dee have risen in proportion with Mark's popularity, and he has since had a model named after him. The original 'Supernatural' design came out in 1978.

The band bought an old Leyland van and enough gear to make live work a viable proposition. Mark and his father put an old coach seat in the vehicle and built a partition for equipment. The van could do 50 mph flat out and the only way it could be started was by placing a two-pence piece across two contacts, which would result in showers of sparks. The front-seat passenger got the worst of it. During a journey the radiator that was on the left-hand side of the cab would boil over, spewing rusty water onto whoever was unfortunate enough to be sitting there. Despite that, it proved to be a real home from home and was much used during the following year.

They headed for the sanctity of the Isle of Wight to prepare for their first professional booking – at La Babalu Club. As the big day approached, they were quite obviously nowhere near ready. 'Appearing live on stage on Friday and Saturday, September 5 & 6, Level 42. London's latest disco/soul band' read the advertisement in the *County Press* on 30 August. Polydor Records sent down Maurice Gallagher to monitor the band in a live environment. Hyped up with nerves, they charged through the set. As Mike remembers: 'Suddenly it was the end of the concert and it was as if we hadn't even started it, we were so full of adrenalin. But I think Maurice Gallagher liked what he heard, even if the audience were somewhat non-committal.' They all had completely different stage gear for the occasion. Mike, in his naïvety, presumed that if you were appearing on stage, you had to wear something loud in order to project yourself. As a result he bought himself a tiger-striped satin jacket and striped trousers.

Boon remembers the gig as being fairly mediocre, the audience consisting mainly of large gaps and the odd friend dotted about. 'One of them said he liked my rhythm playing as if to say he thought my lead playing was crap. I'm sure it was but I didn't need telling.' Their musician friends were less than enthralled. The highlight of Boon's evening was when he spilt a pint of beer down the front of his new light-brown trousers.

Boon recalls Maurice as being a 'very genial Irishman' whose favourite saying was 'Shall we retire to the bar, chappies?' It's doubtful that they needed much persuasion.

Level 42 found themselves caught up in the new wave of British jazz-funk and being lumped together with bands like Shakatak, Linx, Light Of The World and Central Line. They insisted that they were not part of any wave and were merely doing their own thing, but they could not ignore their instant following. They did not have to sell themselves as a band or flog round the club circuit to gain recognition. 'I have no complaints about us being lumped into the Brit-funk scene, but musically there was more to us than that,' says Mark.

And Phil was later to tell *Record Mirror*: 'We don't mind being called a jazz-funk band for convenience's sake as long as people realize that we aren't one really!'

John broke the news that Polydor were on the verge of signing them to a five-year contract as they were preparing for their first booking in the South-East at Flicks in Kent Road, Dartford, Kent, on 4 December. They had played at Nottingham Palais on 16 November at an all-dayer promoted by Les McCutcheon of Shakatak. It was something of a disaster, with several girls from the audience commenting to Boon: 'We didn't expect Status Quo.'

Says Boon: 'The problem was that we weren't your archetypal jazz-funkers. When you think about all the influences that had been thrown into the melting pot, there was quite a heavy element to what we played. Coupled with the fact that we used to play everything at twice the speed, it must have come across as mayhem on stage. I suppose it didn't help having long hair, as the fashion then was the short-cut, clean look. However, the word was getting out about this amazing new bass player called Mark King.'

In an interview with the *Daily Star*, Mark said: 'Half-way through our Nottingham gig, a guy at the side of the stage held up one finger, so we assumed we were on our last number. We rushed off, then found that the signal meant we were going down a bomb and should carry on!'

In fact the band, and other funk outfits in a similar vein, had trouble being readily accepted north of Watford for quite a while because Brit-funk was a southern trend emanating from London and incorporating the Home Counties. The North was at this time heavily into soul, and Level 42 made inroads across Europe before they began to conquer the North.

They prepared in earnest, knowing that they had to be good. Thursday 4 December came round and Flicks was heaving with bodies. The adrenalin again pumping through his body, Mark played like a man possessed. 'It was nerves that made us play so fast,' admits Mark. 'Someone once told me that the worst thing you can ever hear on stage is silence, so rather than not let people laugh or respond, you do something about it. We just used to go for it, and even to this day I can't talk in a relaxed manner between numbers.' The night was a great success. But not for Boon. Two days before, he had been cutting a length of polythene with a rusty old knife and had sliced through a finger. He received seven stitches and ended up playing wearing a bandage.

In the audience at Flicks was Paul Fenn of the Asgard agency, who had been invited along by John Gould. He recalls: 'There were no vocals apart from on "Love Meeting Love", but it was a good show. Immediately after, that record entered the charts so we decided we would work with the band. We booked odd dates around England. They had a large following on the underground circuit so we had no trouble booking them in. The only trouble we had was in developing new areas.' The south of England was never a problem, and Paul would work hard to convince club owners in the Midlands and the North that Level 42 were a crowd-puller. Slowly but surely headway was made.

'(Flying on the) Wings of Love'/'Wings of Love' had been released by Polydor as their follow-up single. It shot into the disco charts and peaked at 76 in the national charts.

The release of the single put Mark in the hot seat for his first personal appearance. Accompanied by Mike Lindup, the scene was a Soul Weekender at Caister-on-Sea, north of Great Yarmouth, Norfolk. Running the show, on the site of a caravan park, was Funk Mafia deejay 'Froggie'. A biting cold, easterly wind blowing off the North Sea had not deterred several thousand soul freaks. Mark was frozen in his shoes – and not just because of the weather conditions. He was in a catatonic state. The problem was that he hadn't even sung on the record. That had been down to Mike. At the scheduled time, they shuffled nervously on stage and, as the song hit the turntable, they began to mime. Mark decided to execute the 'Slosh', the only dance he knew, continually slapping his leg for effect. No doubt the following morning he awoke nursing a sore leg alongside a bruised ego.

On Saturday 13 December, Level 42 played Southall White Hart. The following Friday/Saturday they appeared with UK Players at the 12th National Soul All-Niter at the Centre Ballroom,

Farnham Road, Slough, before retiring in high spirits to their respective homes for the Christmas festivities. They had finally signed to Polydor. There was money in the bank and they had the backing of a major record label. They had the feeling that 1981 was going to be a good year.

Chapter Nine
Love games

On New Year's Day, Level 42 were on the road again, appearing alongside the UK Players once more and Eddy Grant, at an all-dayer at the Lyceum, Wellington Street, Strand, London. Two days later they appeared on Robbie Vincent's Radio London programme 'special' entitled 'Where Do We Go from Here?'. Robbie took a candid look at 1981 and discussed potential future developments with Level 42 and other guests including Light Of The World, Linx, Eddy Grant, UK Players and Freeez. Suddenly, Level 42 were on the treadmill.

On 24 January they popped up at Rafers club in Manchester. 'Back by popular demand, the fabulous Level 42' appeared at Flicks in Dartford ('the home of British funk') on Thursday 12 February; on Thursday 26 February, Level 42 were live on stage at the Queensway Hall, Dunstable, with Mirage; on Sunday 1 March 'top Brit-funk band Level 42' were at the Embassy Suite, Balkerne Hill, Colchester; on Saturday 4 April they appeared at a jazz-funk soul all-dayer at Harrow Leisure Centre.

Brit-funk was slowly but surely taking a firm grip on the nation. It had taken over the disco dance floor and new bands were popping up every week. Several members of Light Of The World, who had been caught up at the beginning of the explosion, found one line-up too restrictive and splintered into the two groups, Incognito, and Beggar And Company. Linx had blown the charts apart with their hugely successful 'You're

Lying'; Innervisions, from Manchester, were in the disco charts with 'Mr Mack'. Level 42 found themselves riding on the crest of a highly popular wave.

In March 1981, Polydor teamed the band up with producer Mike Vernon and they recorded 'Love Games', switching studios from the Vineyard, off Sanctuary Street, central southeast London (now PWL [Studios] owned by record producers Scott, Aitken and Waterman) to Chipping Norton Recording Studios in New Street, Chipping Norton, Oxfordshire, owned by Mike Vernon. They say the Vineyard is haunted. It certainly is according to Mark and Phil. They were relaxing over a game of pool when suddenly one of the balls shot across the table of its own accord and into a pocket. That was their cue to run into the control room screaming their heads off!

'Love Games'/'42' reached number 39 in the charts in April. *Blues & Soul* reported: 'This is a definite winner within the first four bars, during which time Mark lays down one of the hardest and most fluid bass lines of the year that acts as the firmest of foundations for the whole song. It took a couple of listens for me to fully appreciate what a good record this is.' *Melody Maker* commented: 'Superior jazz-funk . . . The bass is phenomenal, bubbling and bursting like nobody's business, the hard funkified guitar riff's a treat, but the middle section is a bit of a bland let-down. This has style though and is exactly what Freeez, who are too careful by far, should be looking at. Class and dance.' *New Musical Express* was not so kind: 'A lot of people are influenced by the ideology and the immaculate textures of supermarket muzak these days: Level 42 are chained to them. Their idea of a 12-inch single is a three-year coma recorded in seven minutes – huge yawning gaps of music and Clearasil-coated vocals.'

The band suddenly found themselves on *Top of the Pops*. 'I can't really remember doing it, although I can recall thinking how small the studio was,' says Mike Lindup. 'On television everything looks glossy and big, when in fact the stage sets are tiny and tacky. Leroy Williams was on congas. We wanted to make a good impression. The miming part was something else! Doing TOTP was like wearing a feather in your cap. I'm sure we were walking around thinking that everyone was going to recognize us. They didn't.'

Boon hated appearing. 'I always felt shy on stage, which I eventually got over, but it was a disaster for me in those early days. I could hardly move, literally inching from side to side. On television you really have to exaggerate your movements.'

As the re-bookings flooded in, Level 42 went back into the studios to record their first album for Polydor. In the meantime, Andy Sojka had been trying, albeit unsuccessfully, to get Polydor to take over the tapes of the unfinished tracks which he still held. He had already paid the band the small royalty they had earned from 'Love Meeting Love' under the Elite label, and any further monies that would have been due to them had the album – provisionally entitled *Strategy* by Andy – been taken up. It meant that Andy had to sit on the record with his hands tied, as he no longer held the rights to 'Love Meeting Love' or 'Wings of Love', which were to be included on the album. Polydor at the time had no intention of including the tracks on the band's forthcoming album. Andy asked the company if he could have them for the album that he was intending to release, and they agreed, much to his surprise. He duly went into the Playground Studios in Camden Town, spent three days mixing the tracks and got Atmosfear's bass player, Lester Batchelor, to design the sleeve.

As this saga was continuing, Polydor had released the second single, 'Turn It On'/'Beezer One', in July, which reached number 57 in the charts, and their first album *Level 42* in August, which received favourable reviews and eventually climbed to number 20. Vince Moren summed up many people's thoughts when he wrote in *Sounds*: 'Although in a live situation Level 42 leave a lot to be desired in terms of stage presence and actual life, they make damn good records. Sometimes soothing, occasionally passionate, they represent the acceptable side of jazz-funk, be it British or American . . . Criticizing Level 42 is hard because they are so enthusiastic about what they do and this enthusiasm is channelled into their performance.' Mike Vernon had managed to capture the essence of the band's live sound with its highly charged funk rhythms and moody vocal lines.

'The album's success stunned everyone at the company, apart from one or two of us who believed in them anyway,' recalls Alan Sizer, who worked in Polydor's A&R Department as a general manager and was responsible for Level 42's output up until the *World Machine* album in 1985. 'When they were signed in 1980 there was this Brit-funk movement going on and there were a load of new British bands. I wasn't the kind of man who went to discos by choice. I went to them as part of my job. We had a manager who had a finger in every pie, playing a marketing role, basically, called John Perou, who used to organize and market this material. I told him, "It seems to me that there's a new thing going on out there. I'm not in a position to plug into it but you are."

'John specialized in dance, soul and black music and he and the club promotions man, called Theo Loyla, concocted a plan whereby they put the word about that we were looking for material, and to bring in any likely looking bands that had been recorded on independent white labels. It sounds quite mechanical but, as it turned out, it was a very valid way of working.' In a short period of time towards the end of 1980 Alan had found Second Image, Level 42 and Shakatak. He had also come across Linx but by then his boss had said that enough was enough.

The activity on Level 42 had been quite prompt but even after 'Love Games' the company looked upon them as merely a part of the Brit-funk scene. They were essentially a dance or jazz-funk act and the reasonable ceiling for their singles was about number 40 in the charts. According to Alan Sizer, people presumed that once they got there, the steam would run out. In fact the success of 'Love Games' took the steam out of everyone else. 'It was at that time that the first glimmerings started to appear in people's minds – mine included – that the band might actually be doing something,' admits Alan.

In the meantime, Mark and Phil had been doing their own thing. Level 42's rhythm section had been drafted in by saxophonist Gary Barnacle and Ross Middleton, former leader of Positive Noise, to play bass on their funky love song 'Cash Flow', one of the demos that helped secure them a contract with Epic under the name Leisure Process. Mark was torn between the two outfits. 'I wanted to leave Level 42 at the time, as it had all been at the cottage industry stage for so long. We didn't know any better, so why shouldn't it have been that way? I can't apportion blame. Gary Barnacle had asked Phil to play roto-toms and myself bass on a certain track because he was getting together with Ross Middleton. It worked out so well that we talked about forming a band. Phil and I told CBS that we had our own thing going as Level 42 and were signed to Polydor, but if they made it worth our while we would do it. In fact Muff Winwood saw us about it. Polydor got wind of what was happening and Alan Sizer from the company told them to leave off. Leisure Process was exciting musically. If you haven't done anything, then there is nothing to leave, and Level 42 by this time hadn't achieved anything.'

Mark went down a similar route four months later when Jeff Beck inquired as to his interest in joining himself and drummer Simon Phillips as a three-piece. Mark had several rehearsals with them. He liked Jeff both as a guitarist and a man. 'The best musicians I have met, none are precious about it,' says Mark. 'We didn't get it together because, unlike earlier in the year, something was starting to happen with Level 42. It was all going along much nicer.'

After appearances at the Middlesex and Herts Country Club (12 August), Hull – Beverly Hills Disco (14th) and Brighton – Sherrys (16th), Polydor planned a tour to coincide with the album release, which began at the Venue, London, on 21 August and took in St Albans Civic Hall, Norwich – Penny's, Braintree – the Barn, Preston – Clouds, Neath – Talk of the Abbey, Scunthorpe – Tiffanys, Scarborough – Tiffanys, Burnley – Tiffanys, and ended at Haywards Heath – the Taverners. Present at the Venue gig was Alan Coulthard, writing for *Record Mirror*. He noted: 'The dance floor which, from being somewhat redundant, gradually became more populated as the unsuspecting punters fell victim to the lure of the insidious, irresistible groove. By the time the band launched into "Turn It On", the dance floor was packed with shuffling, gyrating bodies . . . From here on in Level 42 should go from strength to strength.'

Riding on the waves created by their eponymous debut album, Level 42 were offered the support role to the Police on their seven-date tour of Germany. It was September 1981 and the band were in the process of winding down their highly successful promotional tour of England. Only forty-eight hours before they set off for the Continent, they had delighted 300 fans on a hot autumn evening at the Taverners in Haywards Heath, Sussex. Germany was to be the band's first real initiation into the rock and roll circus. They were on a high – but before too long would come back down to earth with a bang.

Phil decided to have his hair dyed blond especially for the occasion. A true Sting clone. As they piled their equipment into a Mercedes 307D truck, it suddenly struck them that this was so far removed from where they could ever have imagined themselves at this early stage in their careers. But be that as it may, with manager John Gould leading the way in his Ford Granada, off they set. It was 13 September.

Crossing Belgium and the German frontier on their first trip to Europe as a band, they found themselves unavoidably delayed en route and subsequently arrived in Stuttgart behind schedule. To the south-east lies Böblingen, where they were due to play at the Sporthalle before 5,000 expectant Police fans. They eventually arrived ten minutes before the doors opened. They hurriedly unloaded the van, humped the gear on stage, set up and plugged in. It was only then they were informed that there would be no time for a sound check. Things didn't augur well. Neither did it help their cause that none of the posters in the street announced that there was a support act on the bill.

There was no time to worry about that now. It was time instead to take centre-stage. As the lights dimmed, the audience went crazy. This was the night they had long been waiting for. To see their heroes, the Police, live in concert. The lights blazed. But as suddenly as the Sporthalle crowd had erupted in cheers, it fell deadly silent. Just who were these four Europeans, dressed in their dreadful, shiny club outfits, with their shabby equipment? They soon found out.

It was quite obviously not going to be Level 42's night. The sound was awful. There was no getting away from it. They were dying a death, or more likely a thousand deaths. Sections of the angry crowd started booing, at the same time bombarding the stage with any objects that came readily to hand. Money rained down from all directions. Boon, standing still in his customary stage pose, with head bowed over his guitar, suffered the ignominy of a choc-ice plump on the top of his nice new hair-do. Worse still, Mark, furiously slapping away on his Jay Dee, was the victim of a firecracker, which lodged in the crook of his right arm. As it started to go off, he thought he was being shot.

At last, breathing heavy sighs of relief and feeling totally disconsolate, they shambled off stage with their tails between their legs. 'We were really depressed,' recalls Phil. 'One of the members of the Police entourage came up to us back-stage and said, "Don't feel too badly about it. Our support bands quite often get this treatment."'

'There was a kind of manic energy in the band. We controlled it but it must have sounded awful to the people watching,' reflects Boon. 'It wasn't annoyance on our part, because everything was all together.'

As for Mark, this show more than anything snapped them out of the British club vibe of not really caring about your audience. In fact Level 42 did care, but the venues they had grown used to were far too small for them to gain any kind of projection. 'We were drawing everybody's attention to the stage and keeping it there, because you can do that in a club but not in a large arena. As a result, we went on stage at Böblingen to a thunderous silence.'

'Being out there on stage that first night was like another world to us,' says Phil, 'particularly with the huge lighting rig, a mega PA system and huge amounts of people working for the Police. At that time we were having to hump our own gear, although we had a couple of people setting up for us. In some respects John [the manager] was wrong. We should have got used to the idea of such a large scale of operation early on but John wanted to keep our feet on the ground. As a result, through the whole of 1981 we packed up our own gear.'

Mike Lindup remembers that at that time roadies were a luxury and John was running a tight budget. 'We were quite happy, though, although it was hard work. A lot of people never imagine it is. They hear your record on the radio and automatically presume that you must be a millionaire and are waited on hand and foot. The first thing I discovered was that chart success doesn't mean fame and money.'

After such a débâcle, it was decision time for the band. They were determined not to be a party to such a humiliating spectacle ever again. Out went the stage outfits, to be replaced by jeans and T-shirts. They pared the set down to thirty minutes, throwing in all their fastest numbers (in those days even the numbers that were fast on record came across twice as fast live anyway).

That first night back at their hotel, the band let off steam. Mike was off to bed as the others bribed the doorman to open up the swimming pool. Splashing around, Mark and Boon thought it would be fun to throw the furniture into the water. Phil stormed off thinking how silly they were being. Perhaps they were, but after their calamitous gig, they could think of no better way of making a splash.

Following the nightmare of Böblingen, they travelled to Essen, where things took a decidedly better turn. The head of the German sound crew went on stage at the beginning of the concert and announced that the Police had some special guests from England who were going to appear on stage first. It was all Level 42 needed. They went charging out on stage and for the first time in his life, Boon decided he was going to try and move around, just in case there might be any more flying choc-ices winging their way in his direction. It was Sting's birthday, so Mark started to sing 'Happy Birthday'. That immediately broke the ice. 'Clap along!' he shouted, and the response was immediate. Things were beginning to click at last. They realized exactly what they had to do to motivate such a large audience – not only project their music, but themselves into the bargain. They had learned the hard way but it had paid off – almost.

The final gig was at the Olympia Hall, Munich. The crowd

responded superbly until the last song when Mark said: 'Good-night, Heidelberg.' It went down like the proverbial lead balloon. Fortunately the German promoters were impressed overall and asked the band back to headline their own tour before the end of the year.

It was an exciting time all round. Things were finally beginning to bubble. High spirited, and more often than not high in spirits, they found it difficult to suppress their enthusiasm for all things rock and roll. After all, wasn't this what it was all about? Staying up all night, getting pissed, socializing with whoever happened to be around at the time? So they generally made a damned nuisance of themselves with their school-type pranks. Only Mike abstained, preferring to retire to bed early, and sober, with other things on his mind – and hanging on to his arm. 'Everybody used to say how boring I was because I used to go to bed. My weakness was women,' admits Mike. 'Suddenly you were desirable. It was always a standing joke that there would be thousands of groupies after our first night, but of course there weren't really. I used to go to bed early because I didn't drink or smoke and there was no point in hanging around where everyone else was.'

Boon remembers those sessions well, as well as the drug scene. 'In Germany people were hanging around with cocaine and they used to give us some, which we had never had before. We thought, "This is great", but after four days we would be going out on stage knackered and couldn't play, so we more or less knocked it on the head before it got too silly. As the touring progressed, we became very hardened and tried to maintain some sort of sanity. It's difficult because you get so lonely on the road.'

The German promoters were keen on showing the band some-thing of more specialized entertainment. Inside one private club, they were handed a towel and a key, which they naïvely accepted. 'Apparently you had to take all your clothes off, put them in a locker and place the towel around your waist,' says Boon. 'We giggled inanely for five minutes. Phil left claiming it wasn't his scene but the rest of us stripped down to our Y-fronts and put the towels on. The next stop was a sauna, a hot plunge then a cold shower. I wasn't having any of that. Besides, there were loads of naked Germans running around. We moved to the bar where we sat and drank beer feeling decidedly stupid in our brilliant white towels, being chatted up by ladies wearing brief tassles. The German promoter and our tour manager were having a whale of a time.

'After a few beers I decided I had to try it just the once. Her name was Stephie. She left me in this room with this dreadful muzak playing, dim lighting and a plastic sheet on the bed. I removed my towel to display my orange Y-fronts. Then she returned, stripped off and lay on the bed. It was all too much for me, what with the muzak and the dim lights, so nothing happened. She made an easy £50.'

Heading back to England after appearing before a total of 45,000 people on the Police tour, the band stopped off for three concerts in Holland, including an appearance at the Paradiso in Amsterdam on 12 October, which, with 1,200 present, was a sell-out. They also did a television recording of the single 'Love Games'. Mike Lindup remembers: 'The Paradiso was very much *the* gig where everyone plays the first time in Amsterdam. It was an old church which had been converted into a rock venue. Three groups were on before us. I had never smelt so much dope before. I must have been high by the end of that concert! The audience were really fired up and it was great. We made such an impression that the album *Level 42* was an overnight success.'

It was at the Paradiso that Mark was to first set eyes on his future wife, Pia, who was the girlfriend of one of the promoters. She was taking photographs to make a poster of the band. Two days later, in Cartouche, Utrecht, they were introduced. They next met while the band were recording 'Love Games' for the Dutch 'Top of the Pops' programme. Mark wrote on a guitar string packet: 'I love you Pia.'

On 23 October the band commenced their first major British tour at Brunel University, Uxbridge. The 22-date tour culminated at London's Hammersmith Palais on 22 November. Pia turned up with two friends, Nancy and Ria and they went backstage to meet the band. *Melody Maker* journalist Steve Sutherland wrote of the Palais night: 'Their lame but successful first album translates into a live dancer's dream, pummelled into furious fits and starts by the best Brit rhythm section in the business – Mark King, bass, and Phil on drums.' Other journalists criticized the band for their break-neck 'speed-funk' approach. 'Level 42 to my horror attack their jazz/funk with such a venom that it puts some heavy metal bands to shame,' wrote Lyndsay Wesker.

Their final single of the year was 'Starchild'/'Foundation And Empire Parts 1 and 2', Released on the 23rd, it charted at number 47 after indifferent reviews. *Record Mirror* called it 'light, filmy jazz-funk; very little but rather insubstantial', while *Black Echoes* slated it: 'Cool, jazzy, classy and cosmic – so why so boring? Must be something to do with the song – that feeble and disinterested melody line.'

During November, the independent record label Beggars' Banquet issued a double album entitled *Slipstream – the Best of British Jazz-Funk*, celebrating an official British Jazz-Funk Fortnight. Included on the release were Level 42, singing 'Turn It On', Freeez and Light Of The World.

In December, Level 42 returned to Europe, taking in four-teen dates between the 6th and the 19th in Holland, Belgium and Germany. It was a particularly bad winter, with tempera-tures down to minus ten degrees, and Boon and Mark took it in turns with the regular driver behind the wheel of the van. The personnel included John Gould, 'H' Griffiths (sound), Steve Thornecroft (sound), Paul Selwood (lights) and Alan Butcher (driver/PA/lights).

The single 'Love Games' had reached number 5 in the Dutch charts. Their first gig was at the Lantaren, Gouvernestraat 133, Rotterdam. Staying at the Hotel Centraal, Kruiskade 12, Phil and Mike shared room number 5, and Mark and Boon number 6. On 10 December the band did a live broadcast on Tros Radio in Dronten. Rehearsing between 4 and 6 o'clock, the doors opened at 7. The soul show ran from 7 till 9, with Level 42 on stage from 9 till 10. The following night they played at Circustent, Olympic Stadion, a large tent in Amsterdam. The power supply was dodgy and cut off on three occasions. Phil ended up filling in with a 15-minute drum solo each time, with Mark and Mike banging cowbells. Church bells may have begun ringing in Mark's ears by this time, as who should show up during the tour but

Pia. They spent some time together as the venues led through Brussels, Wageningen, Aachen, Bonn and – on the 19th – the Evenementenhal, Borne, between Enschede and Hengelo. Mark invited Pia to join him in England in the New Year. She didn't take much persuading.

Chapter Ten
Living it up

The last few months had proved so hectic for Level 42 that they started 1982 with the prospect of recording their next album and no new product to speak of. Their confidence had been boosted by the successes of the previous year, and they felt they were ready to take over the studio and produce themselves. With this in mind but with little other idea of how they would proceed, they buried themselves away in London's Eden Studios with engineer/producer Nick Launay to lay down a couple of tracks.

In the meantime, Andy Sojka was still trying to sort things out with Polydor over the master tape that he still possessed. With the Midem festival only days away, he had set up a distribution deal with Pinnacle and, because of the band's earlier successes, Virgin had placed an advance order of 1,000 copies. Andy received a call from John Gould, who said that he was slapping an injunction on the record as Andy did not have the rights to release it. Andy's immediate reaction was: 'OK. Try it.' At the time he couldn't have cared less as such an action would only have meant further notoriety for Level 42.

The two spoke again later the same day, when Andy stated that he was going to Midem where he would license the album to all and sundry. It was by no means an idle threat. John inquired if they could come to some sort of an arrangement, and Andy suggested that if anyone wanted to resolve the issue, it was going to cost a lot of money. 'How much?' was the reply. Off the top of his head, Andy stated he wanted £25,000, bearing in mind that the album had probably set him back £8,000 in production costs. This was becoming more personal as the minutes ticked away. Pressings were already lined up and raring to go.

The day before Midem, Andy was invited to Polydor to collect his money. In good faith he took with him the sleeve artwork. 'They wanted to put the album out as a thank-you to their fans because they had a very good live following and the fans loved Mark's playing,' says Andy. 'He was playing some of his most raw stuff then so it was a good commercial decision.' The album, *The Early Tapes – July/August 1980*, was released in March and went on to chart at number 46. The sleeve work handed over by Andy Sojka presumably ended in the bin, as Polydor styled and packaged it their own way. Says Andy: 'Level 42 are the most unlikely set of people to be superstars because there is no image apart from the sleeve artwork. I wouldn't have become involved with them if they had sounded like Shakatak, which to me is like housewife jazz. Level 42 are jazz-rockers, which in some respects is an awful term. They had the songs and they had that ability with melody which is probably what sustained them. But the bass lines they ended up doing were too fast and frantic. Jazz-funk at the time implied the Crusaders, Ronnie Laws and Spyro Gyra. Theirs was a much more raw thing.'

In April Polydor released 'Are You Hearing (What I Hear)?', 'The Return of the Handsome Rugged Man', which charted at 49. The single received airplay on Radio 2, something the band could have done without when dee-jay Terry Wogan back-announced Level 42 as Junction 42!

The band were proving enormously successful throughout Europe as they prepared for an extensive tour which was to culminate in two sell-out shows at London's Hammersmith Odeon. The German leg of the tour began on 18 April at Audimax, Aachen, and took them through a total of ten stops, finishing at Alabama Halle, Munich, before they got their first breather – a day off. After three dates in Holland, they played a further three in Belgium before appearing at Captain Vidéo, Paris, on 5 and 6 May. Level 42 then made a triumphant return to the UK where they played twenty dates on the trot, starting at Manchester University and ending at Hammersmith Odeon on 31 May.

Paul Fenn was capitalizing on their appeal, and rightly so. 'The groundwork that had been developed was starting to pay off. There was always a reluctance, as there is with every act that plays any kind of dance music, to play a seated venue, but in terms of prestige you have got to do it eventually. The Hammersmith Odeon is in a class of its own because they don't restrict the audience – they can stand up. Everybody had this thing about holding back from going into the Odeon, but having done it, it was then a case of, "Let's play Wembley!" '

Still high on their success, the band were reunited with Mike Vernon, who was to take over the production of the forthcoming album *The Pursuit of Accidents*. They had tried to do it on their own, it hadn't worked out, and they were happy to admit it. Says Alan Sizer: 'The band's strength in one sense, but weakness in another, was as an improvisation unit both individually and collectively. They could write a number that was a very valid and full-blown tune from the slimmest of ideas because they were fertile in both cases.

'An instance of what could go very right or wrong was after the first album which was produced by Mike Vernon. They decided that they didn't want to be produced by him again, which was actually a provisional decision because they ended up doing *The Pursuit of Accidents* with him. They had written some new numbers – the first ones I had heard for about nine months. One of them turned out to be 'Eyes Waterfalling', which I thought was one of their clever numbers off the album. It was jazzy and complex.

'They had spent about ten days in the Maison Rouge Studios – the first few days to warm up and improvise, and the latter days to work on the important numbers. At the time the sessions were finished, the numbers were not. John Gould brought me on tape a rough version of what they had done and it was already apparent that the one they had spent the longest amount of time working on was the most uncomfortable, the most laboured. Far too much mental work had gone into it. The track they had just busked on for half a day for the B side wasn't complete melody-wise but the feel of it was lovely. Theirs was very much a way of working that I got used to.'

More often than not improvisational numbers in the rehearsal rooms would be simple, strong and full of potential but by the time the band entered the recording studio, maybe a month later, they could not leave well alone. The tracks would become complex, purely because they had had too much time to live with the track and they couldn't resist the temptation to jazz it up. There were forces in the band keen on not being too commercial as it would perhaps damage their reputation as artists. According to Alan Sizer, this meant more to Phil than any other member. 'If you pushed them too far on doing a single or something conventional, you would hear, "We're Level 42. We don't do things like that." '

Level 42 were conscious of the need to move away from the instrumental format that had stood them in such good stead in the past. They wanted to introduce more vocals into the act, both in the studio and on stage, with the serious intention of dislodging the Brit-funk tag that had hung around their necks for far too long. They believed they had the potential to be more original than that and wanted to make their mark as an individual band rather than for a particular sound that encapsulated so many others. They valued their status as musicians, which still sold their records, even if not in huge quantities. Says Alan Sizer: 'There were lots of bands with whom it was far more of a problem from the point of view of the record company because singles had to be produced that would sell records, however much that meant going against the grain or compromising. It can be a real problem. In the case of Level 42 I was lucky, as it would have been down to me had they needed to be forced in round holes or coerced into being commercial.'

Level 42 were doing quite nicely as they were. Their reputation was building, as were the sales. It was important that they discovered how to be commercial on their own terms, without stopping being Level 42. If any stronger external pressures had been applied by the likes of Alan Sizer or other record company executives, they may well have had a deleterious effect in the long term. It was important that Polydor allowed them to find their feet and grow naturally.

Alan Sizer remembers: 'John Gould and I went to a really bad night in preparation for *The Pursuit of Accidents*, when we were trying to encourage the band to get themselves a producer, because there were still these contradictions between themselves as to what they were doing and where they were going. The gig we attended was at the Limit Club in Sheffield, which was not a very large place. The venue had been booked before Level 42 started to grow in popularity and play larger places. Surprisingly enough, there weren't that many people present. The band were standing on a two-foot rostrum and you could jump and touch the roof with your hand.

'They played well and then we struggled to find somewhere decent to talk in Sheffield and ended up in a greasy kebab joint where we had this totally depressing conversation about the production of the album.

'It is evident that they lost their way with *The Pursuit of Accidents*, which is really at the bottom of the pile in terms of my preference anyway. It was mixed and confused and they didn't know what to do. They had had a good time with Mike Vernon but they were wrong to work with him a second time. Then again, it was a case of the better the devil they knew than didn't. They had tried with Nick Launay and it hadn't worked, and the tracks he produced had to be largely remade.'

After a thoroughly disgusting meal they all climbed back into the Mercedes van and headed up the A1 bound for a gig at Durham the following evening. Arriving at a motel at 3 o'clock in the morning, John and Alan managed a fitful couple of hours' sleep before forking out £25 for a taxi to transport them back to Doncaster in the pouring rain. At the railway station, Alan downed a pint of lager and promptly threw up. 'There was this whole thing about how they were going to make it and the problem of producers, partly made by me in the sense that it is the record company man's job to sort out the right person. It is sometimes something that bands resent because they think you feel they are not capable of making their own albums,' says Alan. 'From my point of view the best kind of producer is the one who fits in best with the band's strengths and weaknesses, and can also organize. Basically he is the hub of the wheel. Mike

[Vernon] was recommended in that sense because he was a fan of the band and also because he was able to take what was there and get the most out of it.'

The sharp end of the process for Alan Sizer was in trying to get Mark to realize that he wasn't just one member of the band but that he could, and should, play a stronger role. It was a specific problem in the early days because neither Mark, Mike nor Boon showed any interest in being present at the mixing stage of the tracks. There would an engineer and producer present and Mark's feeling would be: 'As far as bass playing goes, you can't tell me anything about it. This is what I do and I am the judge of what is good or bad. As far as mixing goes, I simply do not have the skills. I am bored with it by that time and I would rather that the professionals moved in.'

On the other hand, Phil would insist on being at the mix, which often proved a functional, rather than a political, problem. A drummer's yardstick for what a band should sound like is somehow bound up in what he hears when he is sitting behind the drum kit on stage. Level 42 would often sit around in a studio and improvise – these jams more often than not turning into recorded songs – and Phil would interpret the music in a different way. Because of this, the engineer would find himself doing strange things to the vocals and guitars to please Phil's ear, and it would be difficult not to overcook the mix. This problem led Alan Sizer to suggest to Mark that he play a more prominent role behind the desk.

The tracks that they had recorded earlier in the year were remixed alongside new material and the album was completed in July. Level 42 took a well-earned rest for three weeks while plans were drawn up for yet another exhausting tour which was to last three months and take in the UK, France, Switzerland, Austria, Holland, Belgium and Germany. Mark and Pia's romance had flourished and they were married on the Isle of Wight on 6 August. Phil took up windsurfing and Mike and Boon 'disappeared'. But not for long. They were soon back out on the road.

On 9 July Mark and Mike had released a single through Polydor, under the names Thunderthumbs And The Toetsenman (pro-nounced Tootsieman), called 'Freedom'/'Freedom A Gogo'. Even if it was all a bit of fun, the breezy Latin-style rhythm had caught the mood of the summer. 'Freedom' stemmed from an idea that Mark had brought to rehearsals following the 'Love Games' single, but it had not been picked up on by the other members.

The Pursuit of Accidents was released in September and stormed into the Top 20, peaking at 17. Released simultaneously was the single 'Weave Your Spell'/'Love Games (live)', which was specially remixed at the Power Station studio in New York. It charted at 43. Despite its chart placing, the album was not without its critics. Karen Swayne in *Sounds* wrote: 'The problem with this kind of sound is that the more technically expert and polished the bands become, the blander the end product and, although the Level lads aren't even close to Shakatak for utter monotony, there's the danger that they're heading that way . . . I don't know whether they are limited by the form or their own imagination, but only by taking a few risks can Level 42 realize their true potential.'

Paolo Hewitt in *Melody Maker* had undoubtedly picked up that Level 42 were undergoing a radical change in their thinking. 'Level 42 are now writing pop songs!' he wrote. 'With melodies! Structures! Middle eights and all that jazz. Level 42 seem to be getting nearer by the minute to a perfect blend and with the whispers in the air insinuating that Earth, Wind And Fire might well be getting involved at a later stage with the group, then Level 42's masterly musicianship coupled with a simplistic pop approach could well turn into a pursuit of excellence rather than accidents. At the moment it's definitely worth investigating.'

Paolo's ear had picked up some sound vibes about Earth, Wind And Fire. While on tour in Germany, the band had been listening to a tape of Level 42 on the tour coach and liked what they heard. Larry Dunn and Verdine White contacted John Gould and expressed an interest in producing their next album.

If *The Pursuit of Accidents* had pleased the punters, it hadn't overly impressed the band members. Phil Gould thought it was very 'dodgy' and even more fragmented than the first album. 'In fact it's probably the most fragmented album we did because we just had bits of ideas. Some of the tracks are just bloody awful. Having said that, *The Pursuit of Accidents* has quite a nice melody to listen to. 'Chinese Way' is about the best thing on it and 'Eye Waterfalling' is fantastic to play live on stage.'

This is where Level 42 proved so confusing to their fans. The numbers they created in the studio never sounded the same on stage. Says Phil: 'In those days we used to have so many bits and pieces in the numbers, like slow intros, manic first verses, breaks in the middle, cuts in the tempo and things like that. The music lent itself to the live feel. Maybe it was not so hot on record but on stage it was great. We didn't fit into a mould at the time. We were supposed to be a jazz-funk band but we didn't play like one. I think it annoyed a lot of people. The Press couldn't nail us down and a lot of journalists, particularly in the minor league, hated us because we had abandoned that way of thinking. They felt we had betrayed black music, yet we hadn't gone the other way. They wanted to call us a jazz-funk band but they didn't know how to make us fit that profile, so it was bizarre really. It was obvious that we weren't going to get a very good Press.

'We had a black music sensibility as opposed to a white rock sensibility. We would tear into the music on stage with a nervous energy, as if we had to get the set over. In the studio we were more controlled and laid back. On stage the adrenalin brought out the white European heaviness. That's what grabbed people's attention. They could never make us out because there was this confusion about where we stood because we never stood in one corner.'

This adrenalin-packed fast style of live play certainly haunted the band and they found it difficult to control. Allied to this was the fact that their success came soon after the demise of punk. Other styles came to the fore such as the new romantics. [It was very unhip to show any sign of competent musicianship after punk.] Any sort of display of musical virtuosity was derided as showing off a technique purely for the sake of it. Level 42, however, were writing material that proved their competence. Suddenly, people found themselves drawn to the band and particularly the speed and dexterity of Mark's bass playing. Some of the Press reviews were cutting and hurtful but, even so, the band were growing in popularity. If they had a good concert and everyone enjoyed themselves, so what did it matter what appeared in print?

Says Mike Lindup: 'On the single 'Wings Of Love', which I wrote and sang, it was very rough and the voice was double-tracked. It was not such a problem in the studio but when we went live, singing it was horrendous. We weren't used to the fact that live you don't have this controlled sound and it is very hard to hear your voice. There was also a fear of not wanting to sound bad in front of an audience so I would try and not look at them as I was singing. In the early years we were criticized for the vocals being very rough and ready, then we started to develop. We did a lot of live work and, as a result, the singing improved. It also became apparent that few instrumentals got into the charts so we thought that if that is what it takes, we would write songs.'

The title track, 'The Pursuit of Accidents', had started life as a fifteen minute jam session with the idea of producing it as a B-side track. It was edited down to the more acceptable length of seven minutes and worked out well. 'The Chinese Way' from the album is very much a Level 42 favourite, and plays an integral part in their live set to this day. Like Phil, Mike was not happy with the finished product, seeing it as too segmented. It was also recorded in about five different studios. 'We were still very much involved in the musical arrangement and had very strong ideas about how we wanted to develop the songs. We used Mike [Vernon] again but we weren't quite as happy as the first time. The general opinion among us was that it didn't work out as well. The album didn't have the flow that *Level 42* had, and I suppose that was quite a hard album to follow. We didn't realize at the time that people look very hard at you the second album round.

'The cover was awful, which didn't help!' confesses Mike. 'We used this artist (Joy Barling) for the first album and that worked out well. She had this idea for the second album of a rainbow coming out of a drain with broken glass but it didn't look that good and there was a horrible photograph on the back, with us sort of smoking. They didn't use smoke, though; it was a type of incense – tons of it, and again the idea of light shining out of the drain. We still didn't really know much about creating an image for a band and it didn't concern us at all.' Polydor tried to team them up with a fashionable photographer but the band only had a vague idea of what to wear. They tried to keep the look simple with T-shirts. It wasn't until much later that they started to realize the benefit of a good image.

Level 42 followed the release with a mini tour of the UK, taking in seven dates between 11 September (Guildhall, Portsmouth) and 17 (Central Hall, Chatham) before storming through Europe yet again, taking in twenty dates between 28 September and 18 October. They visited France, Italy, Switzerland, Germany, Austria, Norway, Sweden, Holland – where Mark celebrated his birthday and was presented with an enormous chocolate gâteau in his face – and Belgium. In the middle of the tour Mark and Pia became the proud parents of baby Florrie. Upon their return to Britain, the band began a sell-out tour on 3 November at the Regal, Hitchin, Hertfordshire. The fan mail was pouring in. One letter came from an ardent supporter and bass player who wrote to Mark from Bremen: 'I know you have heard this from many people before me, but I tell you nevertheless that you are for me one of the best players on the bass in Funk-Musik.' This was from a fan who had seen the band on no less than five occasions.

Present at the Hammersmith Odeon booking on 7 November was Sally Gethin, writing for *Melody Maker*. 'Level 42 were impeccable . . . They played fourteen numbers in all. Each was a winner, and never did the enthusiasm and vigour of audience or band flag. Twenty minutes into the set and nearly everyone was on their feet, unable to hold back from Mark King's legendary and captivating bass guitar work.' It was an impressive night indeed. The band also received an outstanding reaction from their three Scottish dates, playing Glasgow, Edinburgh and Aberdeen.

As the Christmas festivities drew closer, Level 42 were invited by Larry Dunn and Verdine White to meet them at their studio complex in Los Angeles. The future was shaping up nicely. They had often expressed an interest in breaking America, and 1983 could be their big chance.

A Christmas card to 'Thunderthumbs' read: 'Have a smashing time, good luck in 1983 – keep the fabulous music coming! Thanks for the great music of '82.'

Chapter Eleven
Standing in the light

On 7 January 1983 Polydor released the single 'The Chinese Way'/'88 (live)'. Co-written with Wally Badarou, who has had a hand in all the Level 42 material either as a musician or producer, the disc brought them their best singles chart placing to date, at number 24. On 28 January the band appeared on BBC Television's *Top of the Pops*, followed by a one-off date at London's Brixton Ace on 3 February, which was filmed for Channel 4's *Whatever You Want* programme. The support was the a cappella group the Flying Pickets. Level 42 were also involved in a half-hour special in BBC2's 'Sight and Sound in Concert' series before flying to Los Angeles in March to begin the recording of their fourth album.

Verdine White had first come across the band in 1981 whilst in London with Larry. He bought all their current material, and developed a particular liking for 'Starchild', off the eponymous album. They hoped to give the band a foothold in the US market. Level 42 were intrigued by the thought of working with two such eminent musician/producers, as well as looking forward to spending two-and-a-half months in California, away from the miserable English weather.

Six weeks prior to their departure, Larry Dunn and Verdine White had been in England on Earth, Wind And Fire business and took the time out one afternoon to hear what Level 42 had been working on. 'What they heard were three bass riffs,' says Alan Sizer. 'They were appalled, especially not knowing the band beforehand (how they worked in the studio) and this was rule number one broken, because you do not use studio time to write songs in. The "Wally factor" came in. It was very much "Waiting for Wally". I remember going down to the studio to listen to "Love Games" and I said there were a few bare bits, and the "Waiting for Wally" syndrome became apparent because he was their guru, very much so in the early days, totally in the later days and not so much in the middle period. His experience, skills and sympathy were valuable and necessary for the middle time. Even though they would write a number under their own steam, there was a gap which was left for Wally to fill in.

'During the middle period he was under pressure from Island Records, to whom he was signed, not to do outside work and just produce Level 42. Also, Larry Dunn didn't particularly see Wally's involvement as necessary. He didn't think much of him, thinking he was slow and finicky. He thought he could get a sound in five minutes which Wally took six hours to get, which was true in a way because he would try and find different sounds which fitted exactly but which also were not being used by someone else.'

Arriving in Los Angeles and steering clear of hotels, Level 42 found themselves a nice apartment block near Venice Beach and quickly adapted to a leisurely routine. Even their chosen residence, though, was not without its bizarre incidents. On one occasion Mark arrived at the Complex studio complaining that a burglar had stolen his passport, toothbrush, toothpaste and aftershave.

An average day would begin by the swimming pool at 10 a.m., followed by a healthy breakfast at a café near the beach. They would arrive at the studio, about a twenty minute drive away, by 2 p.m. and record until 11 p.m., when it was time for talk. The sound stage next door was in frequent use by such acts as Styx, Air Supply, George Duke, Louis Johnson, Herbie Hancock and Jennifer Holliday.

Weekends were set aside for leisure, when they would hire a car and explore the area. Evenings would be spent partying, at which time they would meet the LA set. They tolerated the musicians, but many others they found superficial. Any waitresses who found out they were a British band would set on them in a flash. 'Actually, I'm not a waitress, I'm a singer. Here's my cassette. Will you play it?' they would plead. Then there were those who would sidle up to the band and say how great their music was. Most of the time these people had never heard of them, so that made the group doubly suspicious of their motives.

After a party one night hosted by Larry Dunn, Mark decided on some exhibitionist driving in a Mercury Capri sports car on the 405 to San Diego. The next thing he heard was a police siren and he was unceremoniously slapped in a Los Angeles jail. After a frantic phone call home in the early hours of the morning, it was the guys from Earth, Wind And Fire who eventually bailed him out.

In April Polydor released 'Out of Sight, Out of Mind'/'You Can't Blame Louis', which achieved only moderate chart success, reaching number 41. It was the first track produced for the band by Wally Badarou, and it had been recorded before their visit to Los Angeles. Says Wally, who was to co-produce from their 1985 *World Machine* album to the present: 'It was a tremendous difference for Level 42 to become a singing band when they were so strongly instrumentally oriented. The first albums had been made on grooves and instrumental themes and the band would sit back and say, "What do we sing?" They had a lot of trouble trying to get original ideas. Because I was not a regular part of the band, I was listening to things with a fresh ear and therefore coming up with new ideas.'

Larry and Verdine were enjoying their work and talking through the music with the band. Level 42 had a reputation for being stubborn and often pig-headed, and their producers on occasions acted as referees. Verdine remembers: 'Phil's a very intellectual-type guy and he wanted to be a producer. Mark's of the intuitive type, a practical joker, but he also got down to the music. Boon was always fragile, a very sweet, quiet guy.

'At that time they were not really interested in hit records but I kept stressing the need for them, which Mark didn't like. Mike told me they hadn't come to cut hit records. At first they were afraid they were going to lose the essence of their music, which I don't think we did. It was the best project I had ever worked on.'

As producers, the project separated Verdine and Larry from their black contemporaries. They were suddenly recognized as being able to produce outside their regular rhythm and blues territory, without giving Level 42 an overlying Earth, Wind And Fire sound. They deliberately steered clear of horns and special effects. 'They were great creatively,' says Verdine, 'What I liked about it was that the sound you hear on record is the sound you hear in the studio; it was a very live feel which is very much up our alley. They brought in Wally Badarou, who did some wonderful synth work. It was unique.

'I had admired the work of Level 42 for a while and when the opportunity to produce them arose, it was a great feather for my cap and career.'

If Verdine thought Boon was fragile, neither he nor the rest of the band saw the inner crisis that had been manifesting itself in the guitarist's mind. He was suffering an intense inferiority complex. Apart from his playing in Big Swifty for a while in 1977, he was merely 'doing his own thing' in Level 42. It started out as fun, with him making up the licks as he went along, while slowly feeling his way into the band. 'I didn't get too actively involved in writing, although I wrote the lyrics for "Love Meeting Love". I was not confident and was just trying to hang on and get through it. In 1983 I started writing my own stuff and mucking about in the studio on my own which helped me develop, but it didn't manifest itself until two years later. I became obsessed by it.

'I was part of the music but because I was always a very shy person, even with the guys, I found it hard to assert myself. Mark was so talented and I was just blundering through the whole thing. Level 42 was making a natural rhythm and I couldn't feel it the same as the others but I felt I should do, and do it easily.' The idea of doing one album a year and spending the rest of the time touring to him was a total waste of creative time. He could never write on the road, needing some kind of stability around him. He was resentful about the whole touring scene, despite it being a very necessary part of the band's growth and success.

With only the final mix to be made on the album, in May Level 42 played their first American concert as British contemporary music representatives in the 'Britain Salutes New York' festival, playing at the Bottom Line Club. Announcing the festival, the New York music paper, *Good Times*, stated: 'With music as exciting as Level 42's, soon the US should be saluting this British band in return.' They hadn't played live for a while and used hired equipment for the show. They were hyped up about America and hoped to impress, but they weren't too happy about their performance. Then they found out they had to do another set for the public. They had never done two sets before and Phil, Boon and Mark groaned outwardly as it reminded them of their holiday camp days on the Isle of Wight, when they were playing three sets a night. Only twenty people showed up off the street. Mark's hero, Lenny White, was present, as was George Duke and Stevie Wonder. And so was an elderly lady, suitably drunk, who asked Mark to play an Elvis Presley number for her.

The band were naturally concerned about the level of interest shown and how the album would be received. Polygram, the American arm of Polydor, were wondering how they were going to promote it, and which department was going to deal with it. There was R&B, jazz, rap, country, rock. Into which little box could they place Level 42? The general problem of breaking the group in the States was compounded by the fact that Polygram wanted to compartmentalize them, but couldn't. Add to that company personnel changes, other changes in thought and policy, plus the problem of getting the record releases to run parallel with those in the UK, and the dilemma was magnified out of all proportion.

According to Paul Fenn, in some quarters Level 42 were heralded as the new Average White Band – but the existing Average White Band were very successful in the black market and Level 42 didn't want to be in that market. But, of course, Polygram didn't know how to promote them in any other area. At that time Level 42 had not achieved any hit singles, therefore until they were categorized, they could not be effectively promoted.

'It's very easy to look back in hindsight but at the time it was an awful problem,' says Paul Fenn. 'The record company would say, "Let's send them out with a package act, but who can we package them with?" ' In the end, it wasn't Polygram who released the album but A & M Records, but it had little if any impact.

Leaving Larry and Verdine in control of the mix, with Phil alongside, Mark, Boon and Mike returned to England with high hopes of European success. Upon hearing the final version, though, it wasn't at all what they had expected. 'The sound had changed a bit and some parts had been edited,' says Mike. 'They were trying to get optimum punch out of each song and the best cut on the record. It's always the same when you get used to the song and then you hear it cut. In a way you feel cheated. The problem of working with American producers is that you get a very American sound. Having said that, we had a good time and we didn't regret it at all. It was a great experience and one of the most enjoyable albums to make for everyone – apart from Phil who had to work really hard on the lyrics. Phil writes from the heart and there was Larry wanting commercial stuff so he was trying to tone down, but without toning down too much. He couldn't write on tour, so he was under pressure to write anyway. The lyrics have always been last-minute in the studio, which isn't the ideal way but it's the way it's always happened.'

Verdine told *Blues & Soul* in its 28 June issue that the project had been a great deal of fun. 'It's been fascinating to see Level 42's sound develop here. I think people are going to be very surprised to see what we have been able to do with the band.'

'I have reservations about the album but it was a positive thing to have done at the time,' says Phil. 'There were some good songs on it. My favourite song was "I Want Eyes", which to my mind was the best and certainly the most consistent piece of music we ever wrote. My favourite type of pop song was "Out of Sight, Out of Mind". I was trying to strike a balance between appeasing the Americans and the record company, and at the same time trying to find our own identity. Somehow, later on, I didn't think it was appreciated. I was trying to find a way for us to sing material that was totally different to what anyone else was doing. With "Standing in the Light", we attained that in certain respects. The lyrical content, the way the melody and the sound of the voice on the backing track worked together; I think we made our mark then.' Included on the album were percussionist Paulinho DaCosta and saxophonist Andrew Woolfolk.

'I think we expected more out of it than we got. Larry and Verdine were also trying to find out what the Euroscene and the sound was all about. We both sat there fishing, and ended up with an enormous cod called *Standing in the Light*,' says Mark. 'I enjoyed the project itself but I don't think that what we were looking for, we achieved. But then I'm not sure that you ever do. To the Americans the buck is the bottom line, but you can't get bitter about it because that's the way it works and to an extent we have been quite successful with them. You simply have to play their game.'

In mid-July, the four grabbed the chance of a mini-break before appearing at the Montreux Jazz Festival. The programme director, Claude Nobs, was later to write to Mark: 'Thanks to you this year's festival reached a peak both in the quality of music and in the number of attendees. We would like to thank you and to express our deepest gratitude for you coming to Montreux this year and hope to be able to welcome you again in the future.'

They followed Montreux with rehearsals for their 1983–4 World Tour. Polydor had released as a single 'The Sun Goes Down (Living It Up)'/'Can't Walk You Home' in July. It reached number 10! The single was born quite by accident. The band started playing around the riff and the engineer, sensibly, thought it was a good line and switched the tape on without the band knowing. Some of the gear had already been stripped down and, as a result, the drums were recorded without any microphones on the toms. The keyboards were recorded through a Marshall amplifier. The vocals were thrown in at the end. 'That's the best way to write hits!' says Boon.

The video for the single was shot in a gravel pit in Norwich. Piles of sand were used to obtain an Egyptian atmosphere and, according to Mark, Bunsen burners were placed under the cameras in order to create the effect of a heat haze.

Back in January 'The Chinese Way' was the first recognition of the band as a hit act as opposed to simply a live touring act. The new single consolidated that fact. *Standing in the Light* – which, despite its failure to break Level 42 in America, had contained some classic singles material to maintain their presence in Europe – was released on 19 August and climbed to number 9. Although Boon had contributed little to the album, he was credited along with the rest of the band on 'Out of Sight, Out of Mind'.

Sara Silver, who was working in the International Press and Promotion Division of Polydor Records at the time, was very aware of the growing concern within both the band and the company of how best to market Level 42. Their tour dates had always been successful, but they were not growing as well as they should have done. They were almost at the point of stagnation. To a certain extent they needed a catalyst to shunt things along, to change the direction of their careers. They had to get out of the rut. 'They had a huge fan base in the UK, solid believers, yet were different from what I had seen before with bands like Madness or the Jam. They were of a different class altogether,' says Sara. 'Everybody saw Level 42's potential but didn't know how to deal with it. Mark always had a burning desire to succeed and a total belief in what he was doing. He was the core.

'The band were established in Europe but were not big sellers; they did not have the backing of the Press, who thought they were naff because they had the soul-boy backing. They got better and better but perhaps their potential wasn't recognized. They were not a "cred" band. Phil is a very ingenuous person, genuinely concerned with the world; as a character, Mike is shy, although he has an interesting depth to him; Boon is Boon, one of the nicest people you could hope to meet; Mark's impact is instant; he is very fast on production but music is still a love to him.'

After *Standing in the Light*, Sara tried to sharpen up their profile with special Press conferences. Liking the band as individual personalities had never been a problem, even if they didn't possess 'street credibility'.

With the success of the album and single still in people's minds, the band embarked on the first section of their World Tour, having brought in percussionist Leroy Williams. Commencing in Margate Winter Gardens on Bank Holiday Monday 29 August, the six-week, non-stop schedule ended at Sheffield University on Saturday 8 October. The band kicked off the shows with 'Dance on Heavy Weather', from the latest album, before powering through their repertoire of classics. The hectic programme took its toll on Mark's vocal chords. With him suffering from laryngitis for a week, they were forced to cancel their date at Queensway Civic Hall, Dunstable, on 4 October. This was re-scheduled for 16

December. Mark's illness also meant Level 42 having to cancel the first four dates of their European tour (10–13 October) in Belgium and Holland. With a week off to recuperate after the Sheffield show, the band set off for France, Germany, Switzerland, Belgium, Sweden, Denmark and Finland. By October they had finished recording a television programme for Channel 4 called *Play at Home*, an hour-long special on the band with live footage of their Hammersmith Odeon concert, plus interviews.

Staying at the Hilton hotel in Munich during the European leg of the tour, Mark got up to one of his usual pranks. One of the lighting riggers had an abseiling kit, and Mark, under the influence, decided it would be a good idea to come down the rope from the eleventh floor. He successfully achieved this nine times, on each occasion walking back through the hotel reception area saying hello to the perplexed staff. On his tenth attempt, the rope locked two storeys up and the toilet that the rope was strapped to was breaking away from the wall. 'I was getting ready to die,' says Mark. He was eventually saved by the road crew who backed the tour lorry up to the hotel wall and, standing on one another's shoulders, unclipped him.

Polydor released 'Micro Kid'/'Turn It On (live)' in the same month, which reached number 37, but the album title track, 'Standing in the Light'/'Love Meeting Love', in November hardly made a ripple. On 25 November the band recorded a *Whistle Test on the Road* for BBC Television at the Ace, Brixton, which was broadcast on BBC2 that night and repeated the following evening.

The band returned to the UK in mid-December, beginning a mini-tour on the 13th at the University of Kent in Canterbury and taking in Chippenham, Reading, Dunstable, Croydon, Swansea, Hanley (Stoke) and Brighton. On the 22nd, long overdue for a holiday, they headed home for Christmas.

The seasonal break extended through March by which time Level 42 had signed a new recording deal for the United States and Canada with A&M Records in Los Angeles. On 11 March the band appeared at London's Hippodrome club in order to receive an award at the DJ Convention of Great Britain, who had voted them the Best British Funk Band.

Level 42 were still tired after the hectic schedule. They had become fractious with each other, no doubt through living out of suitcases for so long. They needed breathing space and the New Year offered a welcome relief. 'Through the continuous touring, by the end of 1983 we were going mad and becoming quite irritable,' recalls Mike. 'It wasn't that the relationship within the band was strained, but that we had been stuck in the sardine can for so long.' Mark usefully used the time to write and record a solo album called *Influences*, those influences stemming from such luminaries as Chick Corea, Stanley Clarke, Miles Davis and John McLaughlin. Mark admits that the primary reason for doing the album was because he wanted to buy a house and Polydor advanced him £20,000.

He had a lot of ideas that had lain idle and which he wanted to get down on tape. He was clearing out the cobwebs from his mind. It was an expression of his musical thought processes through Latin, rock and jazz. As far as Polydor was concerned, Mark had earned the chance of a solo recording. 'The company was starting to get the idea that Level 42 were good and Mark King was a potential star, so it was fairly easily argued that he deserved it, and the album would probably be a very good idea. There was an underlying reason in that I wanted to get him into the studio by himself to find out what he could do,' says Alan Sizer. 'As far as I am concerned, it was a distinctive, informative experience. A lot of it in a sense was indulgent in that Mark was getting the dirty water off his chest.'

Mark began the recording using a DMX drum machine as a guide then added bass and guitar, as further guides, to cover the melodies. He then laid down real drums over the DMX, before rubbing the latter out, and similarly with bass and guitar – a time-consuming process but necessary because Mark got the feel of a band performing that way. He played most of the instruments himself as it was the quickest and best way of achieving the sound he particularly wanted. Mike Lindup knew several of the pieces designated for the album since he had often played through them with Mark during the band's rehearsal breaks, and stepped in where necessary. The A side was a single piece entitled 'The Essential'. The B side included the classic, 'I Feel Free', which

Mark had covered as a tribute to bass player Jack Bruce. It was like the repaying of a debt, as the song had had such an effect on him through the years. It was released as a single three weeks before the album, but it hardly dented the charts.

' "I Feel Free" definitely would have been a bigger hit than it was but, like a lot of Level 42 records, got slightly second best by the company, who just didn't set a high enough target. It wasn't their priority. By the time it marched into the charts under its own steam it was a bit too late; the time to co-ordinate a big push had gone. Mark actually took this harder than with any Level 42 record. It was his. He had given it his all,' says Alan Sizer. 'I remember hearing Mark having a conversation with A J Morris, the managing director, about it being practically buried, which showed that Mark was prepared not only to complain to the manager, John Gould, but to anyone if things didn't go right.

'That was the beginning of when Mark realized that things could be bigger and better than they were. He knew the way to do it and that he had to take charge of it. He had to streamline Level 42, give the band focus and make them go in one direction only; he was very single-minded about it.'

Recorded at Marcos Studios, *Influences* was mixed in two days. Mark is a believer in the one-take approach and was conscious of keeping it as live-sounding as possible. It was released on Polydor on 13 July.

April's Official Fan Club newsletter announced that in the *Blues & Soul* awards for 1983, Level 42 had been voted Best British Act – for the second year running. They beat Second Image and Galaxy into second and third spots respectively. In 1982 they pipped Imagination and Central Line. Mark was voted the second best bassist for 1983 (pipped by Marcus Miller). The positions were reversed the previous year.

In between working with Mark on his album, Mike had also been busy writing with Phil, but most of the time they found themselves pulling in different directions. It was only on Wally Badarou's arrival that they started to gel. The band wanted to record the new album in Britain and called in Ken Scott as producer. His credits included Stanley Clarke, David Bowie and Supertramp. Ken, an Englishman based in Los Angeles, flew over for a three-day meeting during which time he heard the material and discussed the project. As he returned to America, Mark disappeared back into the studio to finish *Influences*.

As usual, they only had vague ideas for songs when they went into the studio, but eventually turned the album round in two weeks. The first half was recorded at Martin Rushent's Genetic Sound Studio at Wood Cottage, Streatley Hill, Streatley, Reading, Oxfordshire – a new generation of studio in which Martin had deliberately designed the control room to be larger than the studio itself, with the idea of actually making the album from the control room. The weather was superb and they played tennis tournaments with Billy Mackenzie (of the Associates), who was in the other studio. The latter won!

Level 42 then moved to Parkgate Studio, Catsfield, Battle, East Sussex, to complete the album. One of the tracks they recorded was 'Hot Water', which began life as a fifteen minute jam session. It wasn't until the recording stage that they drew it all together and added the lyrics. The single was edited from the 12", as opposed to the album, version. It was this track that galvanized the band back to the high spirits that had been missing for some months. They weren't overly impressed with the studio, especially in terms of the mixing, as they seemed to hear a different sound when the tracks were played back on tape. But they had enjoyed the spontaneity of their playing, although writing material during precious studio time had grown to become a risky and expensive pastime.

They actually began recording the backing tracks on Saturday 21 April and continued for ten days, before setting off on a festival tour for a month. From 6 to 13 May they were in Spain, and from the 14th to 28th they did an East Coast tour of the US and Canada, including Boston, Philadelphia, New York, Washington, Chicago, Detroit, Montreal and Toronto. They arrived back on 29 May only to depart two days later for Germany to appear at four festivals. On their return, the band went back to Parkgate Studio.

Level 42 had a three-month run of releases shortly afterwards. On 18 August 'Hot Water' was performed on Peter Powell's BBC1 television show, *One on the Road*. Six days later 'Hot Water'/'Standing in the Light (remix)' was released to critical acclaim, climbing to number 18, the pounding rhythm and explosive saxophone playing showing the foursome at their no-nonsense funk best.

> Tell (tell) you something (what)
> Music is the key to set me free
> To the beat (on the street) I'm jumping
> Forgetting all the things they said 'bout me.

The words rang out, almost prophetically.

In September the album *True Colours* was issued, reaching number 14; its tracks marked a definite change in the band's music. In October the single 'The Chant Has Begun (edited version)'/'Almost There (edited version)' reached number 41. The first song title was inspired by a mural on the A&M building in Los Angeles, entitled *The Chant Has Begun*, depicting the St Elmo village in the city – a charity house for needy children, supported by A&M. The mural also inspired a song by the Alarm, entitled 'The Chant has Just Begun'.

Reviewing the album, *Melody Maker's* Colin Irwin wrote: '. . . doesn't fully sustain this exciting new face of Level 42. They still get bogged down in limp rhythms and turgid melodies like the thoroughly dull "Kansas City Milkman"; while on "Seven Days" they drearily turn their hand to the sub-bossa nova mood currently in vogue among all the nouveau-jazz dullards . . . Yet Mark King, at least, is singing with a bite that suggests real conviction and vicious intent, even if the material or arrangements don't always match the quality of "Hot Water" or the electrifying opening track "The Chant has Begun".'

Between 19 August and 2 September, the band travelled to Hong Kong and then on to Japan for dates with the Japanese jazz-funk outfit, Casiopea. Writing to his parents, Mark noted: 'Dear Mum and Dad, Thought you might like a postcard! It is the monsoon period and is peeing down, though it is very hot (about 95 degrees). Boon and I went to Kowloon and are now going into Red China on a tour.'

The monsoon wasn't the band's only drenching. Going over the top in an Osaka disco, the club bouncers plucked them out of the disco's swimming pool and left them drenched and shivering in the cold night air!

Sara Silver remembers Japan being a tricky tour for the band. The country had welcomed Shakatak with open arms, and presumed Level 42 were of the same ilk. 'When Level 42 turned out to be nothing like Shakatak, they [Japanese promoters] slightly turned their back on the band,' says Sara. 'The Japan music scene is rather like that of France, in that no one in the world particularly understands it. Our company were good but obstinate. The kids buy a pop star image, it doesn't matter what your credibility is. You could sell anything as long as it fitted into their vein. Level 42 did not get the break there the first time round. They had to go there to start the ball rolling and then get Polydor on board.'

On their return to Europe they embarked on a promotional tour doing television shows and live concerts in Holland, Belgium, Germany and Spain. It proved invaluable. Richard Skinner, co-presenter of BBC Radio One's *Saturday Live*, went on holiday and invited Mark to stand in for him on 8 September, which he did willingly. The record promotion included appearances on *Top of the Pops, Crackerjack, Saturday Superstore, Dr Mambo, Music Convoy* in Germany, *Countdown* in Holland, Belgium's *Hotel American*, a live concert for Veronica Television in Holland, and a concert before 50,000 people in Barcelona.

By October 'Hot Water' was number 4 in Holland, 7 in Belgium and was about to enter the German charts. *True Colours* entered the Dutch charts at 33 on Friday the 5th. The first eight days of October were spent in a rehearsal studio in preparation for the autumn tour, with Krys Mach stepping in on saxophone. On the 10th, Level 42 flew to Essen, Germany, to rehearse for a Rockpalast live concert, broadcast to over 50 million people. On Friday the 12th the band recorded two shows in Newcastle for British television, *Crackerjack* and *The Tube*. They then dashed to the airport to catch a private jet back to Germany for the Rockpalast show the next day. It was then back to the UK on the 14th and into production rehearsals at the Academy, Brixton, London.

Their UK 'True Colours' tour began on 21 October in Norwich, ending with dates at the Hammersmith Odeon, on 12 and 13 November. During the same month, Nik Kershaw had an album released called *The Riddle*, on which Mark had played bass on the track 'Easy'. On 17 December Mark was in the studio to produce a single for the Nightcatchers, a Birmingham-based funk band signed to MCA Records. After the 21-day sell-out tour, Level 42 spent a further four weeks in Holland, Germany, Switzerland, Denmark, Sweden, Belgium and France. The band's last concert of 1984 was on 10 December at La Mutualité in Paris to a full house of 2,510 fans. The tour schedule in Bridget King's scrapbook noted: '11 DEC FINISH!!' – it was Mark's writing.

With Level 42 achieving new-found status and an ever-growing army of fans, Mark reflected on the past four years and the bad Press when he told Lynden Barber in *Melody Maker*: '[It was] only down to our inexperience. I can look back now and it's not so much the songs as the way we went about doing them . . . This is our first group and it's now four years old. If you're thinking of four albums, there's not a lot of practice at making records, not a lot of experience. Any experience we've gleaned has got to have come from the road because that's what fills up the bulk of the year.'

It may have seemed yet another successful year as far as the public were concerned, but rumbles were growing louder within the band. Boon's insecurity had almost come to a head as the round of tours began yet again earlier in the year. He had a problem on stage trying to relax and had turned to the whisky bottle, downing a bottle a day before the curtain opened. From when he was a teenager he had been able to drink vast quantities of alcohol without it having an outward adverse effect on him, but he knew that the daily intake was doing him harm. He turned more to his writing, finding that it gave him peace of mind, although the drinking continued through the year.

Despite its success, the band were disappointed with the chart position of 'Hot Water', expecting it to go higher. They were also becoming more disenchanted with their manager, John Gould. 'We felt that we were treading water, playing the same places. I guess the idea came to our heads that John had taken us as far as he could,' says Phil. 1985 was going to be no picnic.

Chapter Twelve
Dear John

The rumblings continued into the New Year even as plans were being made for a February tour which would take Level 42 back to France and onwards to Italy, Austria and Spain. In January the band were involved with international Press interviews and making two trips to France and one to Germany to perform on various television shows. In February Mark visited the Frankfurt Music Trade Fair where he demonstrated the Status bass and Trace Elliot sound equipment. Phil bought his first car, a black MGB GT.

Dates for a French mini-tour were confirmed, kicking off on 21 March in Strasbourg at the Palais de Fêtes and taking in Lyon, Nice, Montpellier, Bordeaux and Rouen. It was the first occasion that the band had played in the French provinces and they proved a great success, setting the stage for further dates towards the end of the year.

Back in the UK, they were booked in at Woolwich, London, on the 30th, followed by Reading and Chippenham. The English dates were carried out primarily to record a live double album, *A Physical Presence*, using the Rolling Stones' mobile. The album was released on 19 June and was to climb to number 28, remaining in the charts for five weeks. It was something of a disappointment for the band, bearing in mind their live reputation. The album was not originally conceived as a double package. But no one could decide which tracks should be included and which left off.

Within ten days of the mixing of the album, Level 42 found themselves yet again back in the studio to begin work on their next studio album, this time co-producing with Wally Badarou. They brought in engineer Julian Mendelsohn, who had worked on the Nik Kershaw album with which Mark had been involved.

John V. Roy, writing in *Melody Maker*, said: '. . . Extended bass solos and hand-claps turn good three minute songs into ten minute epics, the kind of thing that's good if you're at the show, but dull if you're just sitting at home.' *Blues & Soul* was more complimentary: '. . . The chaps are heard in the usual fine fettle doing lotsa their well-known stuff as well as some new toons.'

In April *Blues & Soul* carried the news that Level 42 had been beaten into third place by Loose Ends and Sade as Best British Act in 1984. Marcus Miller had also pipped Mark as Best Bass Player.

On 5 May Mark recorded a show for Capital Radio's *Rock Masters* series at London's Duke of York Theatre, in which he spoke about, and taught a student, bass techniques. Around the same time Midge Ure asked Mark to play on a couple of tracks on his solo album.

Boon had begun the year feeling that the next studio album would be the make or break time for the band. He certainly felt he couldn't go on doing the same thing, year in, year out. Brother Phil was going through a similar trauma, although his was on a more personal level. Although they were total opposites by nature, the chemistry between Mark and Phil had been an essential part of the ingredients that made up the success of Level 42. Mark was ying to Phil's yang. Mark was witty, confident, aggressive, totally self-driven. Phil was more often than not in his own dream world. They would often fight each other on stage. Not in a physical sense, that is. There would be an element of competition in their playing. In terms of pure energy, they gave a lot. The rhythm section in any band is the essential driving force. Within Level 42, it was different in that Mark, as the bass player, was in a way fulfilling the role of the drummer. Phil, as the drummer, has to lock it all together in the role of the bass player but he didn't have the freedom that a drummer would have in a normal situation. Boon and Mike would fill out the top line, and Mark would take over the space where the lead guitar would normally sit. It was all very different, and trying for Phil. Structurally, it can't have been ultimately satisfying for either Mike or Boon, as they were more often than not playing fixed parts. Yet, being so different, it caught the imagination of the public, catapulting Mark, more than any other member of the band, to superstar status.

While this was going on, Mike and Boon carried on in their own sweet way. Mike, very controlled, would maintain his well-known even strain. Boon sometimes pulled away, internalizing it completely differently. Mark and Phil were undoubtedly the more vocal of the four. Phil was the lyricist putting forward the ideas and Mark would translate them into song. Half the time Phil felt Mark had little sympathy with what he was trying to say, or that he really understood how his (Phil's) thought processes worked. Mark would take the lyrics and interpret them his way. But there was nothing wrong with that. It was how Bernie Taupin and Elton John had worked for years. To Phil, he was the mouthpiece and the conscience of the band, not Mark. It created a lot of tension between them. It may not have been healthy, but it drove the two on, making them push themselves even further. After a while it became counter-productive. Other things came into play, such as money, success, egos and, not least, management problems.

Phil bottled up his growing feelings of displeasure. He certainly could not talk to Mark about it. To discuss something like that with Mark would be like giving away something – a sign of weakness. 'Mark won't let himself be considered as weak,' says Phil. 'He couldn't deal with being sensitive to somebody else's needs. He is not psychologically prepared to accept the fact that there is another side to his nature, a more intuitive side. He has to suppress that. If he sees it in anyone else, he sees it as a sign of weakness.'

Phil, admittedly, often went off at tangents. He was the dreamer who would come up with the ideas and the titles for the albums. He was living on a cerebral plane and he desperately wanted Mark to become attuned to that side of his nature. There were some very strange psychological games going on. Phil had been at times living in fantasy land, thinking everything was rosy and they

Above: WHEEL MEET AGAIN… Boy racer Boon Gould in the hot seat as he indulges in one of his favourite pursuits *(London Features International).*

Below: COME FLY WITH ME… The intrepid 'Peter Pan' (Mark) and 'Tinkerbell' (Mike) string along to the music at Brighton Centre *(London Features International).*

Above: STARS AND STRIPES...
'Tiger' Mike is dressed to thrill,
while 'Pilot' Phil looks set to fly the
coop *(London Features
International).*

Right: LICK-SMACKIN' GOOD...
Guitarist Alan Murphy, formerly of
Go West, goes through his paces
with Level 42 *(London Features
International).*

Left: A SHINING EXAMPLE...
Mark makes light work of his slap-
happy technique during Level 42's
highly successful concert tour of
1989 *(London Features
International)*.

Below: PRINCE'S TRUST...
Midge Ure (left) was music director
for the all-stars extravaganza,
which raised £1 million *(London
Features International)*.

Left: HAPPY BIRTHDAY TO YOU... Thirty years on, and Mark has his cake in October 1988 *(London Features International).*

Below: AND THE BEAT GOES ON... Drummer boy Phil looking all kitted out *(London Features International).*

Opposite, top right: THERE'S SOMETHING ABOUT YOU... Mark's clowning glory in the video for their 1985 smash single *(London Features International).*

Opposite, top left: HOW DID THAT SONG GO AGAIN?... Mike Lindup contemplates his next move during the 1988 tour *(London Features International).*

Opposite, bottom: STANDING ON THE CORNER... The dymanic duo, caught streets ahead of the crowd in 1987 *(London Features International).*

Right: UNDER WRAPS... The bass supremo indulges in a solo think tank *(London Features International)*.

Left: YOU NEED HANDS... Mike Lindup decides to rest his laurels *(London Features International)*.

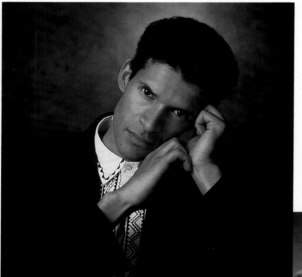

Right: KING OF THE TAME FRONTIER... Mark, captured looking as slick as the band's music *(London Features International)*.

Above: VOCAL SUPPORT… Keyboard ace Mike Lindup has his finger on the pulse *(London Features International)*.

Below: NEVER FELT MORE LIKE SINGING IN TUNE… Mike Lindup in harmonious mood *(London Features International)*.

Above: OLD STAGE HANDS… Level 42 with saxophonist Krys Mach *(London Features International)*.

Below: SHADOWY FIGURES… The band in a studio setting as a statue discus-ses the music with Phil *(London Features International)*.

could all live happily ever after. But not any more. The great divide was yawning before his eyes and he felt himself slipping further and further into the abyss.

The recording of the forthcoming *World Machine* album went smoothly enough at the Maison Rouge Studio at 2, Wansdown Place, south-west London. It was clear that the band knew what they wanted. Mark and Wally effectively produced it alongside Julian Mendelsohn. Says Wally: 'When we decided to do the *World Machine* album, we decided to do it in a more conventional way, with a pre-production period where we would write songs and the lyrics before we went into the studio. It clicked that way. *World Machine* was the turning point. We thought that this would be *the* album. Even before we went into the studio, just by listening to the demos there were already four or five singles we could see. That had never been the case before. We knew they were going to happen, unless there was an accident. Also, the band had become more technologically inclined. A sequencer or drum machine is not there to replace anybody. It is an extension of another instrument. Pre-set instruments are no longer novel. New technology has grown smarter and smarter. It lets the user decide how far he wants to go into the robotic or human aspect of it. We don't use drum machines or sequencers the way artists like Kraftwerk, Jean-Michel Jarre or Frankie Goes To Hollywood do. As much as possible I try and make that technology transparent and let the band be perceived as a band.'

There was no limit to the ideas flowing from Wally, although he has never taken them for granted. It was becoming obvious, though, that those members who were more inclined towards new technology – who were keen to explore all the nuances – had more to say. Basically, it was down to Mark, Mike and Wally. From the outset it had been Mark and Mike who were more willing to use this technology to develop ideas at the first stage. That is where Boon and Phil got left behind in any decision-making, and it no doubt added to their frustration. In fact it is probable that Phil, brilliant in his field, was nervous of losing control to this new-fangled machinery. He no doubt dismissed out of hand the fact that it was something that the band could use to their best advantage, feeling that he was being imposed upon by Mark and

Mike. The album had departed from Phil's love and great feel for jazz–rock as Level 42 strove to achieve a pop band status and he no doubt had a problem trying to come to terms with this new mode of playing. If the heart is not in it, the mind doesn't play ball.

'We had a preliminary discussion before we started the whole project, saying that we were first off going to prove that we could do it ourselves without having a so-called producer, and secondly to prove that we could write songs. We had already proved that we could play,' says Wally.

'In 1985 we decided that we needed to have some hit records. We had been going along quite nicely but the popularity of the band was not increasing and that was a bad sign,' says Mark. 'It was time for a change and we also needed one that would translate to the American market. Phil wasn't happy about this idea but because everyone else wanted to go along with it, he came along for the ride. We set about writing the most commercial album we could and we decided that we would produce it ourselves with Wally. It was quite hard having to sit down with the guys and tell them that I was going to take the responsibility for the album with Wally.

'When it came to the mix we had to tell Mike, Boon and Phil to stay away because otherwise we were going to end up with a compromise, thereby ending up with the same problem as we had with *The Pursuit of Accidents*. It simply wouldn't work. That caused bad vibes, understandably. If you don't get these things out in the open, they have a nasty way of festering. I told them that if they didn't want to work that way, it was fine with me and we could bring in a producer, but we couldn't cloud the issue with compromises. You cannot have a four-way decision. Because of the bad vibes, Phil stayed out of the studio a lot of the time which primarily gave me the chance to just get on and do it.'

World Machine was the last album of their contract with Polydor and with John Gould. John had been given a rough tape of the tracks and the album was fairly well down the line by this stage, the tape having all the songs on the album apart from 'Leaving Me Now'. John didn't like what he heard and thought it a major problem. He didn't think there were any singles present, and was very disappointed. Alan Sizer of Polydor called round at John's

Wimbledon office where John played him the tape before Alan took it away for further listening. 'We had taken the tape to John to get some feedback and he thought it was rubbish,' says Mark. 'He played it to Alan without our agreement, and that was a bad thing to do. It's the same as if I gave you a tape, stating that someone had given it to me and I thought it was awful. When you play it, you are automatically going to presume that you are going to listen to something that is awful. In fact you might quite like it but by that time you have already been influenced. As far as I was concerned, when John did that, it was the biggest nail in the coffin, as it seemed that this kind of negative approach wasn't doing us any good at all.'

As Mark had predicted, Alan's immediate reaction was to agree with John, and he took the tape home to play it through about half-a-dozen times. 'I decided the tape was functional. It wasn't a mixed sound and it seemed nice – albeit suppressed and wooden,' says Alan. 'John was intent on walking into the studio and saying, "Take two weeks out and write some more songs. This is an important album for you", but I said that he shouldn't because the track "Something About You" was definitely a single. I had heard the tape a lot and had got to know the music underneath the sound. I told him I thought the music was a whole lot better than he thought it was and that he was making a big mistake to say anything to the band. The band were self-determined musically anyway, and I know they saw their relationship with John Gould as him doing the management and them doing the music. I went on holiday and towards the end of it I found out that John had actually gone in and thumped the table and said what he was going to say.'

Upon his return from Cornwall, Alan phoned Mark expecting to hear that the recording had gone off smoothly. Instead he got a very excited bass player on the phone.

During the mixing stage of the album, Mark told the rest of the band that he finally wanted to get rid of John as manager, and Mike, Boon and Phil were behind him. They were certainly not happy that John had not worked on breaking them in America, and the problem over money was raising its ugly head. The band basically wanted a better deal for themselves. All four were in agreement. John had to go. They would bring in a new manager. Sara Silver had become involved in the managerial discussions, advising them to find somebody different to John Gould. 'I felt the lid had to come off. Things had to change for them. It was almost too tough to make it work. They had touted themselves to success but you can get stuck with ideas and you don't move on. They had reached the point where they were not growing. It was obvious that something had to give, and John Gould was it.'

Mark, Mike, Phil and Boon called round at John's upstairs office in Wimbledon and told him that his services would no longer be required. The conversation was almost over when Phil, who had often rubbed up John the wrong way – and vice versa – suddenly rounded on him and told him in no uncertain terms why he was being given the push. Mark, being a good Libran, was employing all his diplomatic skills to try and placate his pals in the increasingly tense situation when suddenly tempers exploded and fists flew. 'Phil holds the record for going down the stairs faster than anybody else,' says Mark. 'That meeting showed what was basically wrong with the band, in that you couldn't discuss anything with the Goulds because they couldn't see it outside of a family environment.' An icy calm settled over Mark and Phil's relationship after the meeting. The vibes were far from good, but none more so than within the Gould family who were not to speak to each other for a year.

'It was one of the worst days of my life,' recalls Boon. 'Phil as a child always had this anger inside him and tended to get at loggerheads with John.

'We knew we had made the right decision. We needed someone to take what we had done and sell it. John had become personally involved with the band, and in some ways it was not such a good thing. He was too close to everything.' Boon was inwardly still going through hell. He had split from his current girlfriend and life was steadily going downhill. If he had led a more stable private life, he would have been able to deal with the situation a whole lot better. Even so, after years in the wilderness, he had been responsible with the other band members for an album that was to turn their lives around.

Phil had basically decided that he was going to leave the band.

His communication problem with Mark was still very much in evidence. Phil was trying to justify what he was doing. The most important thing to him was trust and he felt to some extent it was being abused. 'It seemed that whatever I said in the studio was running counter to the thrust or energy of the moment. I felt that every time I said something, I was opening my big mouth, so I just went off to write songs and spent a couple of weeks away.

'I then returned to the studio and carried on but Mark saw it as if I was walking out and we couldn't talk about it. I decided to leave after the 1985 tour. It was very strange. I read something that Mark had said about me and it summed it all up as far as I was concerned. I expected an apology which wasn't forthcoming and I didn't speak to him again. I thought that we would do the tour and then I would go away but it was really bad timing because after that everything took off. Mark and I didn't blow up at each other. We kept it low because Mark doesn't like conflicts. He can't handle them. For me they are the lifeblood of being in a band. You need tension.'

Phil had always had a problem with lyric writing in that he wasn't the type of person who could get up in the morning, sit down and do a job of work. He would always put it off to the last minute. It was a situation that came to a peak on *The Pursuit Of Accidents* and it recurred time and again. Recalls Alan Sizer: 'We actually had to have two studios to get that album finished in time so that overdubs could be done in one and Mark could do vocals in the other to lyrics which were being brought in page by page by Phil who had been sent into a quiet room to write them. The lyrics had been in an area in which I hadn't found it easy to like their stuff from a personal view. I found them a bit mystic, a bit acid rain. It was Phil's style of writing. Some lines, for example, in "The Chinese Way" make you think of lanterns dangling in the breeze, but that was the way he wrote.

'Phil would always look down on Mark as having feet of clay, whereas it was quite easy from Mark's point of view and perhaps from other people's, too, to look up and see Phil in the clouds. There was an insistence in Level 42 that, "We don't do those sort of things" in the early days. Artists quite often use that excuse of, "We're not that sort of band" when all other arguments run out.'

The band went back to complete *World Machine*, with Mark taking a firm hold on things. It was a vital time for Level 42. The album had to be right. Mike could see that it made sense for Mark, Wally and Julian to complete it, although it wasn't the way the band had worked before. Basically, they didn't want too many cooks spoiling the broth. Mark and Wally were full of confidence.

Speaking to Mark at Maison Rouge, Alan Sizer could assess the level of commitment. 'They knew that what they had to do was their best ever album. Mark had taken charge. It was going to be the beginning of his career and he wanted to be rich and successful. He was going for it and nothing and nobody was going to stand in his way. That included John Gould. The slightest murmur from me of any kind which was anti the music and it would have meant me as well. While I was there Julian did a rough mix of two of the numbers, "Something About You" and "Leaving Me Now". It was instantly apparent that John had blown it. They were wonderful. It was quite clear that the album contained hit singles and they had made it. Any slight uncertainty about whether "Hot Water" would be the best dance track of the year was swept away. They had got it right.'

Alan had acted on past occasions as a sounding board for ideas. He would hint at possible single releases of albums, and the band would have their say. He recalls: 'From the early days I used to get involved by entering the studio and listening to several numbers. Although they were run past me for approval, if I disapproved they would probably still be included on the album.

'As far as Level 42 were concerned, I didn't believe "control" was an operative word. There were a lot of discussions about this because people used to see things differently. I remember the managing director used to have a motto which he used to bring out when it suited him, "We should tell our artists, and not let them tell us", to which my reply was, "That must mean that they are not very big as artists because no one tells Brian Ferry or Paul Weller". If you have got to the stage of who tells who, you have already got it wrong. Someone said to me that what is wrong with the music business is that it was an inherent contradiction in words and, if anything, the A&R man is the bridge between the music and the business. If there were times when A J Morris

[Polydor's managing director at the time] wanted more action on Level 42 records, in his eyes it was my job to get a producer, or get someone else to write their numbers, or tell them to be more commercial.

'I spent most of my time fighting a battle to let them do their own thing, with as much support and encouragement to get there faster without thumping the table and laying the law down.' The proof of the effectiveness of that policy is that not following it cost John Gould his job. He tried to lay the law down at an ill-chosen time because he was already under question as a manager.

Near the completion of *World Machine*, a row broke out that Alan Sizer thought was terminal. 'They hadn't finished the drum parts and there was a blazing, stand-up row about the lyrics between Mark and Phil, and then Wally, who had always been Phil's man really. On this occasion he was standing by Mark. Phil stormed off and didn't reappear and they were still recording the drums, percussion, and loads of other bits. They thought, "If he wants to stay away, he can stay away". I was surprised to hear, when they started the world tour at the end of 1985, that Phil was actually playing with them again.' In fact drummer Gary Husband was sitting in the John Henry rehearsal studios at 16/24 Brewery Road, north London, ready for his audition to join the band when he was told that Phil was back in. Mark had been round to see Phil at Mike's request and asked him to stay in the band.

'In retrospect it was probably a bit of a mistake. I could have saved a lot of grief and covered a lot more ground if we had gone straight in and worked with Gary from then on, but Mike was very concerned about having Phil back in,' says Mark. From that moment, it was always touch and go as to whether he was going to stay.

'I had always regarded Level 42 as being four people with individual opinions but working together, that's why it was very hard having the meeting and saying how we were going to go about making the album,' says Mark. 'I couldn't say, "We must do this", because I had no more right than anybody else to say that. I couldn't tell Phil he was out the band, for example, because he could turn round and say the same to me. Phil certainly stayed away from the studio for great periods. Some of the drumming was done with the use of drum machines which also made Phil feel a bit uneasy. I can't really understand that because your role as a musician in a band is that at the end of the day you have to end up with the best song that you possibly can and whatever goes to make that work has to be adopted. Phil just wasn't happy with that kind of recording technique, which is fair enough.

'It's very hard when on the one side you're having enormous success in what you're doing and on the other side the way you're going about doing it is causing such bad vibes amongst the band. All I thought we were doing was achieving what we had sat down to discuss at the beginning of 1985, and that was to have some hit records and make the band much more successful.'

It was probably agreed for good reasons that that was the end of Level 42 as it had been, says Alan, but that they should stay together until the end of the tour, which was going to be a big success. 'I'm not sure who did the overdubs on *World Machine*. Phil didn't come back to finish them so it was probably Mark or Mike.'

In September 1985 Polydor released the single 'Something About You'/'Coup D'Etat'. It shot to number 6. On 9 October the album *World Machine* hit the streets to chart at number 10. Level 42 were accused of selling out to their hardcore fans. The album was certainly far more pop-oriented than any of their previous material, but the fan base was growing, not receding. The sales proved that. 'Leaving Me Now'/'I Sleep on My Heart' the follow-up single, came out on 31 October, climbing to number 15. The band were voted Best Funk Act by British disc jockeys for the second successive year.

'There will always be criticism about us moving away from Brit-funk,' says Wally Badarou. 'The minute you become successful you belong to the public so they decide what you should be. And of course they want you to be conservative, playing what you have always been best at and yet they expect you to come up with something fresh every time. It's a challenge. We felt that there was not much to be said at the jazz level because there were so many other brilliant musicians around. We liked to say different things. Being a jazz-rock player doesn't mean you don't like some tunes by Madonna or Bruce Springsteen.

You like to see what you can do in that area. I believe there is so much I can offer I don't see why I should restrict any of my experiences. It has always helped that Mark has a very clear picture of what he wants musically, so it makes my work as a producer easier.'

Mark told *Number One* magazine in its October issue: 'I won't say we are going for world domination but for the very livelihood of the band it was important that we had new challenges. We only formed the band in the first place because it was exciting, and it is essential to keep that excitement . . . One thing we don't want to do is slice off our roots and say we are not jazz-funks and never have been. We are just trying to say there's more . . .'

Curiously, Phil was to say in the same interview: 'We are not turning our backs on the past, but you have got to move on. We want to make our ideas more accessible to people because we've done some things in the past that have been worth while and should have been heard by a lot more people.'

Paul Crockford and Level 42 were already very much aware of each other. With partner Paul King, he had been running a firm called Outlaw Concerts (later Outlaw Promotions) and one of the acts they had been promoting since 1982 was Level 42. He received a phone call from Paul Fenn at Asgard stating that the band were changing managers and was he interested. Paul got on to Mark and dropped a strong hint. Outlaw were already managing Tears For Fears to good effect. Mark eventually agreed to give it a go. They shook hands over Mark's dining-room table, and the deal was made. There were no ground rules. Paul said he would take on the role for six months. The band and Paul decided to split everything that was earned on an equal basis, twenty per cent each. 'I came in at a fortunate time in that the band had decided that they would work on the *World Machine* album before they went into the studio, whereas previously all the albums had been written in the studio. *World Machine* was much better for it. It was a much more mature record and a commercial one in the nicest possible sense of the word.'

Paul was very much aware that Mark drove the machine and pretty much everyone else that goes along with it. 'He knows what he wants and 99 times out of 100 he gets it. We've had some battles, but we are close, as close as any manager is to an artist. Mark is a very dominent person. He's got an amazing amount of energy. Mike is one of the music industry's gentlemen. He's probably one of the nicest people I've ever worked with. He's very calm, he won't be walked upon but he trusts Mark. That's what happened with Phil. I don't think he trusted Mark's judgement implicitly and whilst it sometimes comes across as being a one-man band, that's far from how it is.'

There was a magic about 'Something About You' that captured the mood of the moment. Suddenly everybody was talking about Level 42. The same thing had happened to Tears For Fears when they released 'Everybody Wants to Rule the World'. In a word, it clicked. Everybody was playing it. Everybody was singing it. In any other circumstance, it could have been just another flash in the pan. But Level 42 had worked for too long to let this moment pass by. They had never appealed to the younger age bracket, the pretty-boys-of-pop brigade. What had happened was that their fans had matured along with the music. At first the group didn't fit the time. In September 1985 they did. The Press may have tried to knock them sideways on occasions, but they always bounced back. Mark had always been up-front and honest with his answers, and it had landed him in trouble on occasions.

There has never been any mystery to Level 42. Usually there was no story to tell. Of course the Press reacted to that. It's very difficult to write about something that is ordinary. That has been much of their appeal. If Mark was not up there on stage playing his heart out, he would be down in the audience with the rest of them. What they did hide, successfully, were the inner torments, the odd bitter confrontation which, to be fair, happens in most bands.

Paul Crockford sat them all down after *World Machine* and lectured them on presentation. They had never bothered to spend time on that side of things and it had always been barely functional. 'Let's go out and look expensive. Let's put on a proper show,' he told them. 'Let's take a risk and spend a little money. Let's have a few moving lights, fly people through the air, explode a few things and make it a bit more of an event.' It had in the past been very workmanlike. Poor Boon would often come under flak for his lack of movement on stage. Try as they might, the rest of the band could not cajole him into the odd shuffle. He was like the Rock of Gibraltar. On one occasion he possibly moved about fifteen steps in all during the show – a tremendous achievement. He was terribly depressed when a reviewer referred to him as a wallflower. He never moved again after that!

Paul had a battle with them about the number of encores they would do. They used to go off stage and return about five times; the audience would love it but the band would be drained. Paul suggested that they play a shorter set, do a couple of encores and leave the audience wanting more.

Mark had dreamed up a strong clown image for the £40,000 video for 'Something About You'. It no doubt helped the single sales, particularly in America, where the video image is more powerful than in Britain. The video featured actress Cherie Lunghi, who had just finished filming *The Mission* with Robert De Niro. Paul remembers that the newspaper *Today* described the band as a 'military precision machine', which pleased him because they had sat down and created their own success. They adopted what Mark termed the 'Rolex approach'. They all went out and bought nice suits to wear on stage and every time they attended a photo shoot they made sure they looked expensive and successful. At last they were pulling away from the unsung heroes syndrome.

On 24 October Level 42 began a UK tour. It was ninety per cent sold out even before advertising began to appear. Starting at Loughborough University, they travelled through Leeds, Sheffield, Manchester, Liverpool, Edinburgh and Glasgow. On 1 November they were at Newcastle City Hall, followed by Oxford, Portsmouth, St Austell, Cardiff, Norwich and Birmingham. From the 10th to the 13th, they sold out at the Hammersmith Odeon. 'Level 42's middle of the road funk clearly fills a gap in the overcrowded music scene . . . In terms of good time rock 'n' soul, they have cornered the market,' noted journalist Terry Baddoo after Hammersmith. But there was always the other side of the penny. 'These days the band seem to be more interested in becoming the Moody Blues of Brit-funk, combining techno-pop

pomp rock textures with the spank-bass funkatronics of Stanley
Clarke. I've had more fun emptying an ashtray,' wrote Frank
Owen in *Sounds*.

On 7 November, a rare day off in the schedule, Mark and Pia's
baby son, D'Arcy, was born, weighing in at 9 lb 10 oz. From 14
November until Christmas the band were off to Europe again.
'Boon Gould and I live the life of dogs for much of the year. We
drink too much and eat all the wrong things. But, interestingly,
we never fall ill. Conversely, Phil and Mike, who are really into
being ultra-fit, are always beleaguered by colds and flu,' Mark
told *Record Mirror*.

Although outwardly enjoying the success, Phil Gould was in
turmoil emotionally. He wasn't talking to Mark, believing that
Mark saw him as the reason Level 42 had not been successful
all those years. 'None of us were seeing the situation for what
it really was. The chemistry within a band is such a rare thing.
People strive all their lives to get that kind of chemistry and we
just grew up with it. We took it for granted and threw it away,'
says Phil. 'We tampered with it and destroyed it. After the "World
Machine" tour, although I was in a terrible state and close to having
a breakdown, having internalized everything and believed it was
all my fault, I went totally into myself. Mike spoke to me later
and we talked it through and I carried on, but it had changed. It
was over. The chemistry had gone. It was a real shame, bloody
stupid really. Our egos got in the way.' In fact it grew so large
in Phil's mind that he met Paul Crockford and told him: 'This is
my band. My place is in this band. This is something I started.
We should try and make it work. Mark came to see me again and
said, "Let's do it", but in 1986 it got worse.' Phil had got caught
up in the flow and found it impossible to back-pedal.

'Level 42 was a different beast altogether and I could understand
him not being comfortable with it,' says Paul Crockford. 'I don't
think it fitted into his view of what Level 42 was all about and he
felt he didn't want his name attached to it any more. I told him
that we were committed to the "World Machine" tour, that we
couldn't blow it or let the people down and he agreed to do the
tour until Christmas. It was a very depressing tour. He was in
a separate dressing room. It was awful. He was going to leave

and everybody was really upset about it. I think Phil felt it was becoming like a proper job and artistically he wasn't happy with it.'

The 'military precision machine' was certainly suffering from spanners in the works . . .

Chapter Thirteen
Lessons in love

'We had a close thing last year where it looked as though Phil would leave the band, but we managed to sort that out. Everyone realized that it was easier to take time to count to ten than make an irrevocable decision,' Mark told *Number One* magazine in 1986.

With Christmas behind them, the traumas that had plagued the band also took a back seat as they quickly got into their stride in January, with television appearances on *Wide Awake Club, Saturday Superstore* and *Top of the Pops*. They also played their debut shows in Ireland before settling down to write some new material for the follow-up album to *World Machine*. Mark had several ideas he wanted to lay down on tape, one of which was 'Lessons in Love', featuring Gary Barnacle on saxophone. When Richard Ogden, then managing director of Polydor, heard it, he told Paul Crockford: 'This is a smash record!' He was right. 'Lessons in Love'/'Hot Water' literally smashed into the British charts at number 3 in April.

Says Sara Silver: ' "Lessons In Love" was the consolidation of their career. "They had had one hit, they had had two hits, let's have a third", was the sudden feeling.

'The album "World Machine" had been like somebody's first album. By the time you get everybody on board to the concept that you have a big hit, and this is all mega-wonderful, the momentum has gone. That is what the rest of the world was a bit like, bar the States.

'The band then come in with "Lessons In Love". It was a question of if you are established and are breaking new ground you have to doubly prove next time round that you are going somewhere.

'I held off [the release of the single] in Europe. I told everybody overseas, "You can't have 'Lessons in Love' ". The biggest warfare blew up and telexes were flying all over. Nobody in the history of the business had quite done it for the reasons I had. There was no awkwardness. The band weren't saying, "You can't have our single". I had been through international product meetings, workshops with people around the world – everybody had come in. I couldn't bear the thought of "Lessons in Love" being lost. I just said, "Until somebody gets off their arse over there and proves to me that the attitude has changed; they [Level 42] have embraced your development, you can't have it". It worked. The German company hated me because they had always outsold the UK. I told them the stakes had just gone up.'

The biggest selling single across Europe in 1986, it was number 1 in Germany, Switzerland and Denmark, number 2 in Holland and 3 in Sweden. 'It was basically Top 5 in every territory in the world apart from America because they wouldn't take it without an album,' says Paul Crockford. In fact, America was quickly waking up to the music of Level 42. 'Something About You' reached number 7 in the American singles charts in April, and acted as a launching pad for the band. Polydor followed up in May by releasing the limited edition US version of *World Machine*. It included 'Hot Water' and 'The Chant Has Begun'.

Level 42 were in America and Canada on a club tour of the east and west coast promoting *World Machine* when the news broke that they were lying at number 3 in the British charts. (Their first booking had been in Toronto, where tickets for the show had sold out within twenty minutes.) They were almost prepared to do a flying visit to record a *Top Of The Pops*. 'We felt it had a good chance of getting to number 1 and perhaps had we been there it might have done so,' says Mike Lindup.

There was an inauspicious start to the tour. They were mostly playing to crowds averaging 300, and would walk on stage to face rows of blank-looking faces. It was only when they launched into the repertoire that recognition sank in.

They had to cut down on some of their equipment due to the size of the venues, and Phil would find himself hidden behind the racks of speakers and amplifiers as they crammed on to the stage. On their return, there was very little breathing space before they were in the studio recording the next album, *Running in the Family*. Mike had taken a weekend off before the recording started in earnest to appear with some friends from the London School of Samba at the Notting Hill Carnival, something he had also done in 1985. Mike played percussion, Brazilian style. 'It is something that you feel rather than learn. You don't read any music. It is a very simple rhythm but to work it has to be played with a certain swing.' Dressed in green striped T-shirt and boater with green ribbon, he joined in the mood of the moment. The stresses of touring floated away for a brief spell.

Mike was well aware of the level of disillusionment that had set in with Phil during the time of *World Machine*, and that the only real communication between him and Mark was carried out on stage. That was as good as it ever was in 1985. As an outsider, you would never have been aware that anything untoward was going on. 'We had made a conscious change of direction. I felt that Phil thought it was a compromise,' says Mike. 'He has artistic principles which are very strong in him, whereas Mark was much more the ultra-professional and realistic one. He saw that if *World Machine* wasn't head and shoulders above the other albums then he would have got fed up and we would probably have disbanded, as we had spent 1983 and 1984 doing nothing but touring and we had not seen much difference in terms of success.'

Basically, Mark wanted to see more of a return for the work they had put in since 1980. He felt they could do better by writing material that was more acceptable to the public. He realized that a good song would probably reach a far wider audience than if they relied on playing ability alone. Mike could sense that Phil wasn't happy with the change, but Mark was the stronger character in that he saw the direction they should be heading and that was the way he headed. Good old solid, dependable Mike had tactfully spoken to them both after *World Machine*. He strongly felt that they had gone through so much to get so far as a band, that if differences could be resolved, it would be worth it, as they were only just starting to realize the fruits of their labours. Often such tensions could prove creative, and *World Machine* was creatively a very good album. It was worth trying to save the band – if it could be saved.

Boon was still going through his own dilemmas, without worrying about anyone else. He was still polishing off the odd bottle of spirits. 'Everything was combining to change me and I started to lose myself.' Among other things, he was still upset over the break-up the previous summer of his long-standing relationship with girlfriend Mary. It was only after the new album that he started to pull himself back together, but that wasn't to last long.

Phil saw it all so differently, as if the whole thrust behind the band was now simply to see how big they could become, how far they could go. The music was starting to take second place and it was all becoming very sordid indeed. Phil was finding it impossible to be creative at any level in that kind of environment. *World Machine* was to be his favourite album, although *Running in the Family* was to spawn a string of hits. But selling records was not necessarily a measure of quality, according to Phil. 'The only thing that some of us were involved in musically was "Children Say" and that is the only time I felt any sort of musical affinity with the album. It just wasn't done right. I still think you can be successful, have commercial success, and still be interesting like Peter Gabriel's "Sledgehammer" track, or Sting's albums, or Kate Bush. There are people that can do it without having to resort to a formula. There is a line in "Two Solitudes" which goes, "Love is lost, I've found, when trust breaks down". I was trying to get a message through, but they weren't listening, or maybe they were but they didn't want to talk about it. When a band gets to that stage it is not going to survive, so obviously it was doomed at some stage to go under.'

Phil didn't think the new album helped their cause musically at all. *World Machine* had been a culmination of the band's musical thrust; *Running in the Family* was like following a set pattern, a reiteration of the previous offering. It may have sold more copies, but he was certainly not proud of it. The ideas presented in *World Machine* had worked and it was a satisfying album to listen to.

Apart from childhood poetry, Phil had written little until Level 42 got off the ground. In 1980 and 1981, having just left the Isle of Wight, writing lyrics was a means of getting his thoughts out into the open. He was still living in a cotton wool world. He was hardly politically motivated, and the only real trauma he had experienced was growing up without the regular presence of a father. But he had compensated for that by living a carefree childhood. He didn't get down to writing about emotional pain until two or three years later. His songs about love were always about the pain of love. He didn't have it in him to write a happy song. There was never any interest in that. He realized that people could identify with the pain and the conflict in life.

By the summer of 1986, he had not spoken to his brother John for a year. A song on the Peter Gabriel album *So*, called 'Don't Give Up' – a haunting duet with Kate Bush – was almost to prove Phil's salvation. He listened to it repeatedly. He desperately needed to hear that song. When he needed a song to vocalize what he was feeling, it was there. So pop music does have its place. If it can be a part of someone's backdrop to a crisis, and helps them through it, then it is justifible. 'What right do I have to moralize?' thought Phil. 'I can't make sense of my own life. How dare I stand up here on my soapbox, my confessional, and carry on like this?'

In both *World Machine* and *Running in the Family*, he had been using the lyrics to relay his message about the demise of Level 42. As far as he was aware, Mark had not even noticed. 'I was writing about the break-up, that inevitability of separations and the loss of innocence and childhood friendships. All those things you have and take for granted when you are a teenager and a young man. The same theme ran through every song I was writing on those two albums, but from different angles. The weirdest thing to me is that I don't think it had dawned on Mark,' says Phil. 'All of a sudden you start saying things and friends that you grew up with don't understand what you mean. You lose the intuitive flow. When it becomes a career instead of a dream, other things get in the way.'

On 5 April, Level 42 found themselves at the Bree Festival in Germany as support to Queen, playing with Gary Moore and

Marillion. A week later Phil was to marry his girlfriend of eight years, Lois, in a registry office ceremony in Copenhagen, where the band were playing concerts. 'We wanted a small, no-fuss wedding, so we had only three guests – our mothers and our son Alex, six, who was "best man",' says Phil, and on 20 June, they appeared in the all-star line-up at the prestigious Prince's Trust birthday party concert at Wembley Arena. On stage between 8.30 p.m. and 8.55 p.m., they followed Big Country and Suzanne Vega. The second half of the concert brought on some of the world's biggest stars: Elton John, Phil Collins, Mark Knopfler, Midge Ure (who was also the music director of the show), Eric Clapton, Tina Turner, Sting, Rod Stewart. It was endless. Along with Mark on bass, the Prince's all-stars got together for a rousing finale, with Paul McCartney on vocals. The night raised £1 million, and people had paid between £25 and £100 a ticket. It was the most memorable rock event since Live Aid in 1985.

The stage and production manager for the concert had been Roger Searle, highly experienced in the music industry and who had previously worked with bands including the Who, Supertramp and Judas Priest on a production level. In addition, Roger was known to Paul Crockford, a member of the Prince's Trust committee. Level 42 needed a tour manager to assist for several weeks and Roger was available. He began working with the band on 29 July. 'They were doing support shows with Queen in Europe. I really only knew Mark and Mike visually,' says Roger. In fact he had Boon thrown out of rehearsals for the Prince's Trust concert because he didn't recognize him. Boon had actually arrived for a photocall and had innocently wandered in. No one had bothered to mention the shoot to Roger. It was not a particularly auspicious start to a forthcoming working relationship.

Having seen Level 42 for a mere twenty-five minutes at Wembley, Roger's first task was to gather them together and check them in on a Saturday morning during the summer at Terminal Two, Heathrow Airport. He was like a shepherd who had lost his sheep. Once they were safely rounded up Level 42 began what Roger refers to as a 'bucket and spade tour'. There were some odd bookings in southern Europe, with outdoor football stadiums in Italy, a strange date in Turin in an area not dissimilar to London's Hyde Park, and shows in Switzerland and Austria. 'Until the first show I did with them in St Gallen (east of Zurich, Switzerland), I didn't realize that I knew most of their material. I hadn't connected the songs with Level 42. That was something they tended to suffer with, particularly in America where, in an endeavour to push their mass public appeal to try to further their career, they would turn up as special guests. People would say, "Oh, that's one of their songs".'

Mark has fond memories of the St Gallen outdoor show. 'We did a lot of festivals in 1986. St Gallen was almost medieval, with camp fires burning in this steeply defined valley. It was very romantic and reminded me of an army on the march. After the Queen support shows we played at Glastonbury at a CND rally. It was one of the nicest shows we have ever done. None of us knew what to expect. Compared to the Queen shows, Glastonbury was quite a cosy little affair.'

Roger Searle's working involvement of a 'few weeks' was extended to the longer term. He took on the role of tour manager at the critical turning point in their career when things were not too complicated. Their first tour of Europe together had involved one bus for the crew, one for the band and two trucks for the equipment. By 1988, they had four buses, three for the crew and one for the band, and five or six tractor-trailers to carry all the gear. It has all been proportional. As they grew, so did the size of the venue.

In 1986 the band were presented with their first-ever platinum disc, which they achieved for the sale of over 300,000 copies of the *World Machine* album. With 'Leaving Me Now' still charting and very much in the public eye, the band spent a brief, but fun spell before the cameras in Dublin in a cameo role for the film *The Fantasist*, starring Timothy Bottoms and Christopher Cazenove. They had been asked to write some music for it and perform one of their early hits, 'Love Games', of which Mark was later to comment to journalist Julie Godson: 'We're actually in the film in this club scene, which is a bit embarrassing! All the other bits of music in the film look really convincing, but we look as if we don't know what we're doing.'

Level 42 had been invited to open for Steve Winwood in the United States, the first opportunity they had had to appear inside

American arenas. Roger Searle had a wealth of experience by comparison, and was almost on home ground at the venue. From 1 October, dates beckoned in France, the USA, Canada and the UK, with Lyon (Bourse du Travail) and Nice, (Theatre de Verdure), Montpellier and three gigs in Paris, McNicols Arena, Denver, Colorado, (the opener for Winwood), Mesa Amphitheatre, Arizona, Universal Amphitheatre, Los Angeles, Mountain View, Seattle Coliseum, Edmonton, Winnipeg, Louisville and Toronto to name but a few stops on a schedule that would keep them out on the road for two months. The American tour went particularly well, reaching its climax at New York's Madison Square Garden where they appeared before 20,000 people. In New York for the show were Paul Young, Genesis's Tony Banks, Mike Rutherford and Phil Collins, and Helen Slater (the actress who had played Supergirl). Phil Collins paid an unexpected visit backstage to wish them good luck.

At Maple Leaf Gardens, a funny thing happened, as Alan Niester wrote in *The Globe And Mail*: 'He [Winwood] literally got blown off stage by the opening act. This wasn't supposed to happen. Level 42 was not supposed to turn the Garden crowd – Winwood's crowd – into a frenzied, squirming mob. It was not supposed to have them joyously bopping in the aisles, and leave them literally screaming for more. But it did, and Winwood could only pale by comparison.' Niester suggested that perhaps Winwood should have hired a 'less vivacious' act to open, and ended his piece: 'Level 42 brought an incredible power and urgency to such dance-floor smashes as "Something About You" and "Leaving Me Now". After last night's display, there is little doubt that quartet's next album will break it wide open.' It was just the boost the band needed at this time.

During what free time they had in America, the band amused themselves by buying and assembling radio-controlled off-road racers (with four-wheel drive). Mark, Mike, Boon and Phil spent every available hour in disused parking lots racing the vehicles in competitions between each other. The overall champion was Mark. Asked about the secret of his success, he commented: 'It's all in the assembly.'

Driving a Ferrari in the hills around Los Angeles during a break in the schedule, Mike Lindup was competently avoiding most of the rocks that littered the road surface. Coming across an exceptionally large one, he thought he could clear it. He was wrong and ended up putting a hole in the engine sump. Nursing his ego rather than his wounds, Mike caused £4,000 worth of damage. He told his fans later: 'I am fine. I have no cuts and bruises. I have had no mental traumas and I am still driving. Thanks to all of you who wrote in; I really appreciate your concern.' Back in Britain, Mike bought a Lotus Elan with the intention of rebuilding it.

The date 30 November and the nights of 1, 2 and 3 December were to be a very special time for the band. Wembley Arena was in sight with sell-out concerts to perform. They drew fans from as far afield as the Falklands. 'Level 42 are the most savagely brilliant pure pop group in the world today,' wrote journalist Mark Sinker in *New Musical Express*.

The show must go on, and between 15 and 22 December Level 42 were in London's Sarm studio with Wally Badarou and Julian Mendelsohn, putting the finishing touches to the new album. It was a triumphant end to 1986. It looked as though the problems with the band had been ironed out. It was impossible to believe that things would change so dramatically in 1987. But change they did.

Chapter Fourteen
It's over

'Level 42 – *Lessons In Love*: "We're young, talented and have eight bob in our pockets," summed up the situation of Level 42 a year after it was founded. Since then, the four English lads have sold millions of albums worldwide, and have been voted Best Group of the Year in the United Kingdom several times.' So read an extract from the official news-sheet of Midem '87 on 26 January. Level 42 had been voted the best funk group of the year in Europe. The year had begun well. In February 'Running in the Family'/'Dream Crazy' reached number 6 in the charts. The New Year had brought no let-up in the popularity stakes. The month was spent on European promotions, rehearsing and recording a German show, popping back to Britain for an appearance at the BPI Awards, then going to Norway and Spain.

In March Mark was involved in the recording of 'Let It Be', the Ferry Aid single released on behalf of the victims and families of the Zeebrugge disaster. Pete Waterman, one third of the Stock, Aitken, Waterman production team, who produced the single, was to write to Mark: 'After all the mayhem of the last few days I would just like to take this opportunity to thank you for your very special talent, your effort and especially for taking the time to make "Ferry Aid" the success that it was.'

The new album, *Running in the Family*, which featured both Gary Barnacle and Krys Mach on saxophone, went to number 2 on its release, achieving platinum status within a week. Yet once again the British Press were hardly impressed. 'There's very little actually wrong with it but you get the definite feeling that Level 42 are just cruising when they could be putting the foot down,' said Ian Cranna in *Smash Hits*. 'Words on the edge of my vocabulary like professional, musicianly and pleasant immediately spring to mind, but after half a dozen plays (how's that for dedication?), I seem to be left with just one . . . and that's dull,' said Peter Kane in *Sounds*.

Never mind. Level 42 had *eight* nights at Wembley to look forward to as part of the British leg of their world tour which was to take them through fifteen countries. The tour began on 24 March with two nights in Birmingham followed by Poole and four nights at Wembley, three in Manchester and four more at Wembley, and then ever onward. As a grand finale, Mark and Mike are hoisted fifteen feet into the air, with Mark still thundering out a compelling dance beat on the bass. Kicking his legs, he swings across the stage as the audience go into a frenzy. It was all caught on video for posterity. As the stage explodes in a shower of pre-set sparks, the audience find it hard to drag themselves away.

Level 42 are a good, fun band for pre-Christmas nonsense, but Mark wisely felt that the winching stunt would have proved too much like a pantomime. Even so, the crew dubbed Mark and Mike 'Peter Pan and Tinkerbell'. 'Mr Peter Pan and Mr Tinkerbell, if you don't mind!' came Mark's reply.

As the Manchester dates loomed, Mike Lindup found himself speechless. He had strained his voice trying desperately to be heard over the noise of the crowd and backing vocalist Annie McCaig, who had become a regular feature of the band's live dates, covered for him. 'Losing my voice was a very frightening thing to happen. I hope it will never occur again. I found myself having to mime some of the parts but it worked out well.' Mike ended up spending three days in his hotel room not speaking to anyone until he went down to do the shows. 'It was frustrating not being able to ring anyone up and having to whisper for room service. Basically I knew that I had to just shut up!' Mike was able to perform again during the second stint of Wembley shows.

The band sold out houses throughout the European tour. In

Zurich they drew a crowd of 12,000 and in Cologne, 8,000. Between dates at Offenbach and Furth, on 13 May the band travelled to Montreux for the Golden Rose Festival, and following the 31 May date in Valencia, which wound up that stage of the European tour, Mark again appeared at the Prince's Trust event. While they were on the road, the single 'To Be With You Again'/'Micro Kid' charted at number 10.

June, July and August took them to America, where *Running in the Family* had been well received, particularly by Rob Tannenbaum. He wrote in *Rolling Stone*: 'Like other young professionals, the members of Level 42 understand that emotional and technical steadiness is a key to success. *Running in the Family* artfully hugs the median of contemporary pop.'

Level 42 had crossed the Atlantic to appear as support to Madonna. According to Paul Fenn, Level 42 had been earmarked for a tour with the Thompson Twins, but after the latter had cancelled their British dates due to poor ticket sales, they pulled out. 'Suddenly Level 42 were up for the Madonna concert, and a week later they got it,' says Paul. 'They were a name act and even Madonna needs an opening act with a name to justify the ticket price and to help sell tickets. The schedule read: 27 June Miami, Orange Bowl; 29th Atlanta, The Omni; 2 July Washington, RFK; 4th Toronto, CNE; 6th–7th Montreal, Forum; 9th Boston, Sullivan Arena; 11th Philadelphia, Veterans Stadium; 13th New York, Madison Square Garden; 15th Seattle, Kingdome; 18th California, Anaheim Stadium; 20th–22nd Mountain View, Shoreline Amphitheatre; 24th Houston, Astrodrome; 26th Dallas, Texas Stadium; 29th Minneapolis, Metrodome; 31st Chicago, Soldiers Field; 4–5 August Cleveland, Richfield Coliseum; 7th Detroit, Silverdome; 9th–10th New York, Grant Stadium.

Musically, it worked fine. But at times they found it difficult. They would find themselves going on stage at 7 p.m. when it was still light and when the stadia were only just starting to fill up with people. It was difficult to get an atmosphere going when they only had forty-five minutes to make a suitable impression with Madonna fans who were more than likely intent on scanning the merchandising stalls for their souvenir goodies. Mike recalls that the band switched the song list around, placing 'Something

About You' second after 'The Chinese Way'. 'Something About You' was the number the audience recognized, and it was usually downhill from there.

The band met Madonna on a couple of occasions, but only briefly. She had her own security area backstage and it wasn't as if they could walk up to her dressing-room door, knock and walk in.

Says Mike: 'We got on well with the Madonna crew. Their stage manager would announce us, "Good evening, California. Are you ready for your Lessons in Love? Here's Level 42. All right!", and the crowd would cheer. It was a fun tour to do.'

Madonna later wrote to Mark: 'Thank you very much for opening up for me during my American tour. I hope you enjoyed it. Best of luck on the rest of your tour! Sincerely, Madonna.'

It was during the tour that Mark decided to knock the bottle on the head. He grew tired of going to parties, doing something outrageous and then regretting it the next day. Says Roger Searle: 'Level 42 are the first band I have worked with where I have had to employ retrospective security. Normally, bands take out security to protect them from the audiences and fans. Security with Level 42 was to protect other bar users from Mark King! At the Mad House club in Hamburg in 1987 our security guy Nigel finished up with a black eye, courtesy of Mark getting into a scrap with someone else. It is fine to go out, have a drink and get legless, but it is not fine for somebody in his position. Some people didn't understand that some of Mark's jibes and quip-making were not serious. They got taken the wrong way.'

Mark recalls the incident: 'The club was jam-packed and there were a lot of squaddies and lager louts around. I was winding this bloke up at the bar who kept on nudging me, by nudging him back. Then he turned round and walloped me and I spun round and hit him. Nigel leapt in and got pushed over. By this time the squaddies had gone and it was Nigel and me against Germany.'

Mark eventually realized the error of his ways in New York during the Madonna tour. After a Polygram bash one afternoon with Def Leppard and loads of drink and jocularity, the band attended a Madonna party the same evening in a chic restaurant with waiters in wing collars and tails. It was held along the lines of a designer do with all the beautiful people of New York in attendance. It was a place to be seen and not heard. Not according to Mark who, having broken his foot a couple of weeks before (during a back-stage tennis game with Mike Lindup in Canada), was hobbling around and making a general nuisance of himself poking people with his support stick. The main problem was that as far as the majority of the guests were concerned, Level 42 was where you parked your Cadillac in a 50-storey car park. Back at the hotel and in between the Polygram and Madonna parties, an intoxicated Mark had decided to cut off the plaster cast on his foot with the help of his trusty survival kit that he wears on his belt.

Today 'Mr Sobriety' admits: 'I had become obnoxious. I'm bad enough when I'm sober, but I had become such a git when I was drunk and it was something that wasn't getting any better either. I was growing worse at aggravating people and was in severe danger of it becoming a problem if I didn't stop. I didn't need to drink and I was not an alcoholic but I was uncontrollable when I had had a drink. It is different but it is as bad. Every day I was having a drink I was getting right out of hand. I decided to stop it altogether after the Madonna party. The root of the problem stemmed from the fact that I'm a very excessive person so, if anything, I go too far or do too much. It translates to all aspects of life and you have got to know your limitations. I can be quite strong-willed on these things; it's not a problem.

'I couldn't give a monkey's about drinking now. I quite like to challenge myself into saying that I made the promise to myself. Not drinking now, I see how it really does screw up people an awful lot. I see how people change when they have had a drink, but I never saw any of this before because I was right at the head of the pack. I see it as a weakness in other people if they can't stop and when they need to, which probably transmits when I speak to them. I can't help them, though, that is just the way I am.'

Recalls Roger Searle: 'The day after the Madonna spectacle, Mark asked me, "What happened?" I replied, "If we're on the first plane home, it's down to you!"

'Having said that, I have never seen Mark drink on a show day. The Level 42 rider calls for one bottle of wine in the dressing room.

He did not want the band to go on stage other than in total control of the situation.

'Mark and I are both Librans and, to that end, we are renowned for being incapable of making decisions. When we do make one, we know we have done the right thing.' So drink as far as Mark was concerned went out the window from that day.

It would infuriate Phil that Mark was so together. Conversely, Mark would become equally annoyed with Phil's laid-back attitude. The word 'rush' was not in his vocabulary. But even Mark's super-efficiency was not infallible. On one occasion when the band was due to travel to Madrid in 1987 for a television show, the courtesy cars dropped the members off at the airport early. It was fortunate they did as Mark had left his passport at home. A messenger was immediately despatched to collect it as the rest of the band employed delaying tactics on the tarmac. Mark made it by the skin of his teeth. In 1988 he missed a British Midland flight to Amsterdam altogether. With Mike Lindup and new drummer Gary Husband safely on board, he happily continued signing autographs in the departure lounge, accompanied by an anxious Roger Searle and guitarist Steve Topping, ignoring the final departure call.

The pressure was taking a serious toll on Boon. Those old nagging thoughts about the incessant touring were seriously playing on his mind. He was openly complaining about how difficult it was to sustain their popularity in a country the size of America, and the fact that 'Lessons in Love' was hardly receiving any airplay. He wanted the band to have a rest. They were wasting their time touring and he couldn't see any progress in it. He wasn't eating properly and easily became run-down. Mike remembers the phrase of the moment from the rest of them: 'It'll be all right.' It wasn't. At the end of the Madonna tour they headlined on the east coast of America.

But it was a completely different set-up. They suddenly found themselves playing the same songs on a stage the size of a postage stamp. The whole show had been condensed to fit the working surroundings and it was more often than not impossible to make it work. Even so, they desperately needed to complete the tour in order to be seen to be playing live in the United States. The club tour proved to be a soul-searching time for everybody. Doubts again began to creep out of the woodwork. The working environment was undoubtedly instrumental in bringing to light some of these inner frustrations.

Boon was gradually going downhill because of his life style. He was ignoring his health by not eating properly and still taking the odd drink. When you are not eating at that level, the drink didn't have to amount to much in order to tip the scales. Level 42 usually take their own caterers on tour, thereby maintaining consistency in the level of quality and quantity of food taken. It is not practical for the band to do so in the States, therefore they were going with the flow, using venue caterers. It was very mass-produced food. If it is Tuesday, it must be chicken. 'Unless you are used to it you tend not to eat,' says Roger Searle. 'Boon wouldn't eat properly at venues. In his case, the whole circumstances were not conducive to good health.' Matters were not helped by the fact that Boon had broken up with Mary and the builders were working on his home in Streatham, London, which forced him to stay with friends whenever he returned to England. He was simply not able to lead a normal life, being almost thrust into a touring situation at home. He was living an itinerant lifestyle and it finally proved too much for him.

Roger took him to a New York doctor and drew the analogy: 'This is a '57 Chevvy which is not running too well. Give it a full service, change of oil and put new plugs in.' The doctor didn't find anything radically wrong with Boon that wasn't curable by a bit of tender loving care and attention. It was a serious question of him being run-down. Boon had had enough.

That was when he suddenly announced that he definitely wanted to stop touring. He was fed up, he wanted to go home and get himself well, and could they find another guitarist? In fact Boon wasn't sure what he wanted to do for the best. In the first instance he simply wanted a break and suggested that they all talk again at Christmas. He had enjoyed some solitude, when he could sit down and put pen to paper. He co-wrote 'Lessons in Love' and 'Something About You', and was later to take an active writing role in the 1988 album 'Staring At The Sun'. His final appearance with the band was on the *Wogan* show on BBC television on 4 September 1987. The song they chose, somewhat prophetically, was 'It's Over'. The single had been released with 'Physical Presence (live)' on the B side in August, when it had charted at number 10.

'The year had started well. The ball was rolling and I came together, then it started falling apart again. I wanted a complete rest, and we said we would give it three months and then see if I wanted to come back, but everyone knew that that was it,' admits Boon. 'It was not said at the time and I wish it had been. Performing 'It's Over' on *Wogan* was a prophetic end to it all. It was a good one to go on. On the actual day the band flew off to Canada, I didn't mind. In fact I didn't mind having left Level 42, I just wish it hadn't happened in such a stupid way really. No one should allow themselves to become that ill. I had been living on hyper-energy for too long and it had drained me. There was nothing left.'

Boon's departure came as a big shock to Mark, who had expected Phil to do something like that, not his brother. On learning of Boon's desire to leave, Mike was concerned they wouldn't be able to find a replacement half-way through a world tour, but his doubts were quickly dispelled. The name of Paul Gendler cropped up. Paul was the guitarist for Phil Saatchi, who had supported Level 42 on their British and European tour in 1987.

The last thing Mark, Mike and Phil wanted to do on their brief spell back in England before continuing the tour through Canada and the west coast of America, was to pick up an instrument again. Instead, they gave Paul a cassette of the material, which he sat down and learnt parrot-fashion. Unfair, maybe, but Paul was a competent guitarist and was happy to be included at such short notice. 'He did a brilliant job when we went back on the road in Canada,' says Mike.

Paul Gendler played his role well, but Phil remembers: 'He was nice but he felt bad with me because he was taking over from my brother.' Phil had premonitions that the world tour would end badly. He had been partying a lot during the summer. He did a lot of crazy things he knew he shouldn't have done to his body. Something was going wrong inside. He had been suffering from hypoglycemia (low blood sugar), but did not suspect just how bad it had become. Like his brother, he too was having self-doubts about Level 42, although he couldn't force himself to admit it in any positive sense. 'I couldn't make the decision myself. I could not put my hand on my heart and say, "You have got to get out of this thing and start again". It was eight years of my life. I couldn't let it go so my body made the decision for me.'

On the road to appear at the Maple Leaf Gardens, Toronto, Phil had an anxiety attack. He began hyperventilating. He was rushed to hospital, fearing that he was suffering a heart attack. He thought it was the end. His body had gone. The nervous exhaustion had taken over. Steve White, drummer with the Style Council and a close friend, told Phil later that he knew something was wrong. He could see it in his eyes when he had left to go on the road. He also knew the year was going to end badly. Phil was given some Valium tablets to help calm him, and he was back on the tour coach heading for the next venue. At that moment he stopped smoking and drinking, especially vast amounts of coffee and tea. He completely altered his routine. It was no doubt the worst thing he could have done.

Three nights later he suffered another anxiety attack – on stage. He felt terrible, not believing for one moment that he would be able to get through the night. From that night on, every time he climbed up on stage and sat down behind his kit, he thought the same thing was going to happen. That only made matters worse. He was becoming a complete nervous wreck. He went to various doctors who, he says, prescribed all the wrong medications. 'You wouldn't believe how many emergency units I went to because I didn't know what the hell was going on. I couldn't stop it and yet I thought I was doing all the right things. But apart from suffering from low blood sugar, I had also been taking brewers' yeast every day, not realizing that I was allergic to it.'

Phil, who had by this time told Mark and Mike that he wanted to leave at Christmas, managed to survive the Canadian leg of the tour, but he was obviously far from well. Heading off down the West Coast, they played at the Palace, Los Angeles, during the time of an earthquake. 'We had two gigs, on 30 September and 1 October. We thought the first date went terribly, but the next one, following the quake, went much better. We put it down to the cracks in the building that improved the sound!' says Mike.

What turned out to be Phil's last date with Level 42 was, as he recalls, a 'real hick town' near Dallas. 'That last gig was a nightmare. I was spaced out on Valium. The music was really loud and I could feel my spine tingling. I was beginning to hyperventilate and was thinking, "This is it. I'm going to die", and this was only the third number. It was a bizarre situation. All I could think of at the time was that I was not going to survive the concert yet I couldn't tell anyone what was going on.' It was a sad end for such a highly talented but overly-sensitive musician.

Mark returned to England to complete the mixing of the track 'Children Say'. All proceeds from the record went to London's Great Ormond Street Children's Hospital. Phil in the meantime headed straight into a private clinic in London's Harley Street, where he slept on and off for five days. His adolescent, bohemian life style over the previous two years had almost wasted him. Phil's illness had forced Paul Fenn to hastily cancel the Japanese leg of the world tour. He had received a call from America on a Thursday morning – the band were due to appear in Japan on the Friday evening – stating that instead of flying direct to Japan, the band were routing via Britain as Phil wanted to see a specialist. Paul wasn't particularly alarmed as it wasn't the first time he had come across this predicament. At 5 o'clock that same night he was informed that Phil was being kept in for tests. The tour would have to be postponed. 'I'm sure if the concert dates had begun instead on the Sunday, Mark in that two-day period would have had another drummer and rehearsed him in and they could have honoured their commitments,' says Paul. Within twenty-four hours, a February datesheet with new dates in Japan had been confirmed. Level 42 were to sell out every show.

Roger Searle had been left in Dallas with backing vocalist Annie McCaig, saxophonist Krys Mach, Mike Lindup and Paul Gendler. Presuming that everything would turn out fine with Phil, they set off for Tokyo via Los Angeles for the Japanese leg of the world tour. Roger happened to be the first passenger off the plane at Los Angeles, where he was greeted with the loudspeaker announcement: 'Would Mr Searle please pick up the white courtesy phone.'

It was the band's agent informing him that the Japanese dates had been postponed. The good news was that Level 42 had about ten days to rehearse in a replacement drummer.

Roger had been taking care of most of the personal luggage – 26 cases in all – and managed to rescue all but two before they continued in the hold, bound for Tokyo. All the backline stage equipment had gone the previous day – just for the ride as it transpired, although the fact that it arrived in Japan on schedule was a good enough show of faith. Roger and party switched flights with their baggage, flying Business Class to England on British Caledonian, who charged on the number of pieces of luggage in one's possession, not the weight. Consequently, Roger was greeted with a hefty bill upon touchdown in England.

Mark and Mike visited Phil at the clinic; he was adamant about finishing the world tour. He asked his doctor, who said: 'You can, but you'll probably collapse.'

Phil had once thought his body would hold up forever. 'In many ways I brought it on myself. If I had had the courage to deal with things, and if I had left Level 42 at the beginning of 1986, I would probably have been able to get through without this trauma but I couldn't see the wood for the trees. It took 1987 to make me wake up to the fact that there is life after Level 42. When you are in a band you think it is your whole world. When you put it in perspective, it is not really that important.'

Mark suggested that it would be better for Phil if he stayed where he was and concentrated on getting better. If he continued the tour, he could collapse at any time, and that wouldn't be good for any of them. 'I was thinking on the run and I said to Mike that I wasn't prepared to fold up on Level 42,' says Mark. 'I really wanted to keep things going and if he was up for it, then that was great. If he wasn't, I wanted to know because I was going to keep going anyway. When we saw Phil in the clinic, I suggested bringing forward his departure date because it was a ridiculous situation. I told him, "Let's just say we had a really good time and that's it".'

Phil reluctantly agreed and Mark and Mike went in search of a replacement drummer. They found one in the shape of Neil Conti, a member of Prefab Sprout. He was available and willing. As support act on the forthcoming Tina Turner tour, the set would not be as long as usual, making it easier for Neil to learn the relevant numbers.

Paul Crockford likened the scene to the toppling of a deck of cards. First John Gould, then Boon, now Phil. With Boon, it had come as a complete shock, although he didn't want to land them in a spot and as a result said he would carry on until they found a replacement. Phil's illness had been steadily building up, although Paul was far from amused when it climaxed on the eve of the Japanese tour. First there were three Gould brothers, and then there were none.

The gruelling schedule soon took over their lives again. Neil tried his best to fit in with Mark's bass lines, but it can't have been easy. Both Neil and Paul Gendler had been told that Level 42 would continue on the road until Christmas and then the situation would be reviewed. The Tina Turner tour comprised similar-sized arenas to those Level 42 had appeared at during the Steve Winwood tour the previous year. If anything, they found the tour was on a more mature footing than the Madonna spectacle.

They had grown used to the overnight travelling through America; their luxurious coach was fitted with front and rear lounge, including video and stereo, and beds in the middle. The driver was Gary Puckett from Springfield, Missouri, a former drummer. A country boy at heart, he would be talking to his trucker buddies on the CB, with the radio blaring and him singing along. On board were Mark, Mike, Paul, Neil, Krys Mach and Annie McCaig.

Says Mark: 'Neil Conti did the job and was fine. The band was all right. It was going through the same kind of motions but there was not a great deal of fire present. You couldn't say it was the greatest thing you had ever heard but it was still a band and it was up and running. It was a case of keeping it going until the end of the Tina Turner tour, then I could start a new band up with Mike, Gary Husband on drums and a guitarist he had recommended called Steve Topping.'

Rotterdam was the high point of 1987 for Phil. 'It was strange hearing the crowd go mad. In a way it was as if you didn't have to play any more. They just wanted to see and hear you. You didn't have to prove anything. It was nice that we had achieved something notable and worth while, and it wasn't going to fade away. Even when I felt bad when I came off the road, I didn't believe for one minute that I wouldn't be able to look back at it and be proud of it. It is all part of the learning process, the learning curve in which everything that happened is going to fall into place and have some relevance.

'Maybe Mark and I will be able to talk to each other about it one day. Maybe Mark will be able to look back on things and see it for what it really was and not what he thinks it is now. We live in two different worlds. He'll go on television and say it was an amicable break, but it wasn't. He just doesn't want to rock the boat.

'Level 42 will never be the same again. It will never be anywhere near what it used to be. They'll sell records because Level 42 is a well-known name. They'll tour but they won't further the name now. If they do, they will achieve a completely different level. The chemistry that made me go out on stage has gone. Bands aren't meant to last a lifetime. You've got to move on musically. In ten years' time if I'm not playing drums or any musical instrument it will be for a very good reason. I believe I will always be involved at some musical level. I don't think I'll be able to get away from that in my life, and never want to. There's always going to be that need to be living and learning.

'It's a waste of time if all it comes down to is the fact that you get on stage on an ego trip, you think about your advance and your car outside that turns heads, and you have a big house in the country to show your mum and dad how well you've done. If those end up being the reasons why you make music and carry on doing it, then it is fundamentally unsound. Then again, I'm sure Madonna doesn't have any qualms about playing that game and being seen to be successful. That's the whole game.

'Success at being a musician is to be able to do anything you want to do, in whatever direction you take, no matter if people don't respond to you. Peter Gabriel is like that. He's a real success, yet he has never had to compromise himself. When I saw him in 1986 it really brought it home. I wish Mark could have seen it too, because there is someone up there singing about what he thinks about life and love, and he really means it and he's filling a stadium full of people. You shouldn't be afraid of saying politically sensitive things, such as singing about Steve Biko. It doesn't mean you are going to turn people off. It's quite the reverse.

'The Police album *Synchronicity* was a concept of one of Jung's books, a psychoanalytical concept. It sold seventeen million copies. The track "Every Breath You Take" sold the album, but kids bought the album and it's all like Jung's teaching. You can challenge people with the way they think through this medium. It just depends on whether you are utterly convinced to believe in it. You can only be utterly convincing if you are yourself completely convinced, and only if you totally believe in your own brilliance can you survive.

'Music is a positive force in life. It doesn't matter what level you are on. It can still be something worth while. I've just seen too many people's heads turned by the industry. Mark was one of those people. He probably doesn't think so, but that is why we are not together now.'

Chapter Fifteen
New beginnings

It had been Mark's intention to replace Phil on drums with Gary Husband, who had worked with Allan Holdsworth, Esquire and Syd Lawrence, but Gary was on tour himself until Christmas. Neil Conti had competently filled an immediate need, as had Paul Gendler. Now with Gary available and willing to join Level 42, Mark duly brought in guitarist Steve Topping. On 3 January 1988, the foursome rehearsed at the Warehouse, Lotts Lane, Dublin, ostensibly because Mark and Mike were still spending time out of the UK for tax reasons. 'It was great with Gary. With no disrespect to Neil, or Phil for that matter, suddenly there was somebody thundering behind,' says Mark.

After a two-week stint, they still weren't ready. There was a lot of material to learn and, despite working as hard and as quickly as he could, Steve could only take in so much at a time. As a result the Irish dates were postponed, meaning that the next scheduled stop was Tel Aviv. They stopped off en route in Holland to collect a platinum disc for *Running in the Family* before arriving in Tel Aviv on 20 January, when they were mobbed at the airport. On 23 and 24 January, at Tel Aviv Cinerama, the new line-up took to the stage. They went down a storm.

After hastily taking in the sights and delights of Jerusalem, on their return journey they did Dutch television on 7 February and Belgian television on the 3rd before appearing on *The Late, Late*

Show in Dublin on the 5th. This was followed the next day by a show at Dublin RDS. The following three nights found them in Belfast. Because the Irish dates had been rescheduled, Level 42 could not appear at the King's Hall because a motor show was being staged there. Instead they filled Ulster Hall, to critical acclaim. Then it was off to Madrid for a spot of television on the 15th, and Paris Olympia on the 16th.

The Japanese dates, which had been rescheduled in 1987 due to Phil's illness and subsequent departure, had come around. Nagoya – Kinro Kiakan, was the first booking on 24 February. Tokyo followed on the 25th and 26th, with shows at Shibuya Kokaido and Nakano Sun Plaza, and finally Osaka – Koseinenkin Hall, on the 29th. 'I really wanted to get out and see the countryside, traditional Japan, instead of the technology, lots of cars, terrible traffic jams, and everything huddled together,' says Mike. 'We did the shows and the audience were very appreciative but polite. They would come in and take their seats, and we would put the opening tape on. Normally we would get a cheer for this, but in Japan silence reigned. We would go on and play and they would wait until we had finished and then start clapping. There was no gay abandonment. I suppose it was just their way.'

The band found a complete contrast in Singapore. In Japan it had been cold and miserable. Here it was lush, green, and eighty degrees. After two shows they moved to Indonesia for dates on 5 and 6 March.

Djakarta was an extraordinary experience for them, and certainly one they will remember. Few acts had appeared there before. Shakatak had appeared in the early Eighties, and Tina Turner had also appeared there on stage. On their arrival, the band discovered that the permit for the show had not been issued by the government, and it wasn't signed until 6 p.m. on the day. Driving from the airport, remembers Mike, was a peculiar experience. They passed shanty towns and vast numbers of scooters which resembled rickskaws. They would stop at traffic lights and be offered cigarettes through the window of their car. They were booked into a five-star hotel in the centre of Djakarta, with swimming pool and lush gardens, in complete contrast to the bustling street scene. Because of the problem of the show permit, they had to suffer the indignity of being quizzed by a government committee as to their suitability to play. Recalls Mike: 'They were trying to discover whether we played suitable material and whether we were going to shout something obscene. It all seemed rather insulting. They asked who the group leader was. We said we were a democracy and they laughed at that.'

The shows were staged on the site of an old drive-in movie lot, complete with ridges where the cars used to pull up. In the middle was the stage, surrounded by hundreds of folding chairs. The weather was particularly hot and the crew experienced difficulty setting up the equipment. As a result they brought in some hired help, but it turned out to be very much a Mickey Mouse affair. As the afternoon wore on, the threatening black clouds moved in, but fortunately the rain held off and, much to the band's surprise and delight, the shows went off well. The reviews were good, especially in the Djakarta *Herald Tribune*. It was good for Djakarta, but it's doubtful whether the shows helped sell any Level 42 albums. In Indonesia there is a thriving market in pirated cassettes. Mike Lindup helped boost the black market economy by buying two featuring Level 42.

Announcing details of the band's shows, a newspaper article was headed 'British Level 42 at Drive in Ancol this evening'. It read: 'The four member "Level 42", a British music group, will display their first day of a two-day show at Drive in Ancol Saturday evening. Mark King, the leading singer, told a press meeting here Friday afternoon that they know nothing about Indonesian funs, but added it's interesting to meet with Indonesian people . . . "We will start something here, and we wish to come back," said King, who at the press meeting did not wear shirt. Answering a question, drummer Mike Lindup indicated that their music mixed jazz, rock and classic. He added in the first day show they will play fourteen songs in a scheduled show time of one and a half hours. Asked on why did they choose "Level 42", King said that it's a quite funny group.'

The band had been scheduled to appear in the Soviet Union

between 15 March and 2 April, but these dates had been cancelled. They had been lined up for ten shows in Moscow in a 30,000 capacity venue. Says agent Paul Fenn: 'Level 42 are a very big act in England but couldn't sell enough tickets to do that here. You also have to bear in mind that in England a band does one show and then adds options, but the Russians wanted Level 42 to do all ten. The band would have got bored rigid playing in the same venue for ten days. Then they wanted me to consider them playing five days in Moscow and five in Leningrad. Inquiries then followed about an anti-drugs campaign concert in Moscow on 25 March, right in the middle of that period. It didn't really ring true. They then wanted to move the whole tour forward, and it fell apart.'

The world tour finally behind them, Mark and Mike retired to Dublin, where they were joined by Wally Badarou, to finish writing material for the next album. They transferred to Miraval, which lies inland of Cannes and Nice in Provence, southern France, to record *Staring At The Sun*. The engineer and co-producer was Julian Mendelsohn. Miraval lies in a lovely setting but on this occasion it was beset by problems, apart from the atrocious weather. On various occasions they suffered power cuts. The studio is surrounded by hills and Mark spent what little spare time he had on a trials bike roaring up the tracks. Julian and Mike would take a more obvious route by Range Rover for some fresh air after dinner before returning to the studio.

The album was actually recorded and mixed in three and a half weeks. On reflection, Mark wished he hadn't rushed through the final stages because by December he was back in a London studio remixing the track 'Tracie' for release as a single. 'If you want to write songs, you have to know where they start and finish. You can't do like we always did and make it up as you go along. Touch wood, we got away with it every time but what you end up with are two or three good tracks and a lot of wadding. You have to know how the song goes. If you know that, it shouldn't take you any longer than that to record it,' he says.

Boon Gould had spent much of his time since his departure from the band working on lyrics and was involved on seven of the tracks. The others were written by Mark, Mike and Wally. Gary Husband played drums, Dominic Miller, who had not been around since those first rehearsals in the Guildhall School of Music, played some guitar with Mark doing most of the parts himself. He also brought in former Go West guitarist Alan Murphy on solos. Alongside Gary, Alan has since become an integral part of the Level 42 line-up. 'Steve's guitar playing was fantastic but the personality side was a bit lacking so we tried a couple of other guitarists out before bringing in Alan Murphy,' says Mark.

In July, Mark and Mike took a welcome break. Back on the Isle of Wight, Mark joined a group of Island Venture Scouts on camp at Wootton Station before flying to New Orleans for the video shoot of the new single, 'Heaven in My Hands', which was released on 22 August.

After a round of European promotions for the album, Level 42 were back in the rehearsal studio in preparation for their next major tour, which began with three consecutive nights at the Ahoy, Rotterdam, from 3 October.

The previous week Mark had been anxiously awaiting the birth of his and Pia's third child. Flitting between rehearsals and his wife's side, Mark was happily present when baby Jolie arrived in the world on Sunday 2 October, just prior to the band's departure across the North Sea.

On the first night in Rotterdam they broke the house record, and on the third night they broke it again. The October dates wound through Belgium, Germany, Sweden, Norway, and Denmark. On 11 October Level 42 were back at Boblingen, the venue for their first European date – and disaster – as support to the Police. It was a different story in 1988. November saw them in Austria, Switzerland, Italy and Spain. The band then rested up – all except Mark – for a month before their UK dates in December and through into the New Year.

'The band in terms of vibe is the nicest it has ever been with a new set-up, undoubtedly because the decisions no longer have to be four-way. Mike is such an easy-going person that it enabled me to say, "Let's go underground for eighteen months", without him worrying about it. There was no way we could have done that with Phil and Boon,' says Mark. 'Musically, Alan and Gary are better musicians than Boon and Phil. That's a benefit for a start, in that being in a famous group, you can call on great players to come and join you. There was a chemistry with Boon and Phil, but there is also one with Alan and Gary. It might be a bit different but I think it is probably better than it was before.

'The Level 42 sound hasn't changed that much anyway. It can't have done because I am still there doing it.'

Epilogue

On Tuesday, 6 December 1988, the King family and I were seated around the table eating lunch at Mark's home on the Isle of Wight when the phone rang. It was manager Paul Crockford with the news that the album *Staring at the Sun* had gone platinum (100,000 sales). There was much jubilation as we tucked into another slice of Pia's home-made vegetable lasagna. Mark sat quietly with the merest flicker of a smile across his face. A look of relaxed contentment. And why not? It had taken eight years for the jigsaw to fall into place. Eight long years since he had made the passing comment: 'I would like to return to the Island, buy a farm and run a Ferrari.' There were times when he must have felt that his dream would never come true. If there were he never let them show.

Fortune smiled on the boy who would be King. He now owns a magnificent house near Wootton Bridge, set in seven acres of gardens and paddock. In the garage is an Aston Martin V8 Vantage (Mike Lindup ended up buying a Ferrari Dino). 'I always said I would park a Ferrari in the drive of Joe Butcher, who I used to work for on the milk round, because he used to wind me up saying I wasn't the man that my grandfather was,' recalls Mark. In fact it is his second Aston Martin. He ran the first one off the road in November 1988 while giving a lift to a car fanatic. 'It was a wet day. There was a car in front of me and I wasn't going very fast. The road ahead was clear. I dropped the car down into second, stuck my foot down on the accelerator and this impressive power that I had been talking about leapt into action. The back swung out and the car shot through a hedge. On the other side was a six-foot ditch. I took out a road sign which read "Reduce Speed Now".'

He may not have been fully in control of that situation, but as far as Level 42 is concerned, he has his hand firmly on the tiller, making sure that everything runs a straight course.

At his previous home in Bedford Hill, Streatham, south-west London, Mark converted the attic to accommodate his recording equipment. He has gone a stage further on the Island and had a 48-track Solid State Logic desk installed in a building adjacent to the house. Coloured in soft pink and a delicate shade of grey, it provides him with a perfect setting where he can work at his own pace and without outside pressures to distract him. He finds he has lost patience with studios and now feels uneasy when he is away from the home environment. In the beginning, he had to get away from the Island to make his mark. His egotistical naivety spurred him away from the insular setting, which was slowly but surely choking his ability.

'Although I have always said you can do anything you want if you just go out and do it, I am also very well aware that I was very lucky because as far as I was concerned it was the only opportunity open to me and everything fell right at the time. I didn't start the style that I ended up being famous for playing. It was thrown towards me in that way, in that I was white and doing it. It was racially motivated and in 1980 I was lucky enough for the spotlight to fall on me. That was when bass playing went through the roof and people were saying, "White guys can play this stuff too and here's the man that has done it." Americans would come in to Macari's from time to time and play. Because they were black I used to assume that they must be fantastic musicians, so I always paid attention. In reality that wasn't the case at all.'

Where other musicians and bands have been easy to categorize, Level 42 have been the odd men out. It was always a problem for Polydor Records, who during those early days would say Level 42 and Shakatak in the same breath. By coincidence, both groups would have a record out at the same time and would be lumped together under the Brit-funk umbrella. They were both working in a soul-based area with jazz influences, but in reality they were worlds apart. Try as they might to redefine themselves, Level 42 found it near impossible to shrug off this mantle. When they did, they were accused of selling out. Says Mark: 'I don't think we really lost many of our first wave of fans unless they naturally lost interest. We didn't alienate anybody with the music we released. Because we used to work in a live situation so much at the time, we would be forced to play all of our material anyway because it was the only material we had and we had to fill an hour and a half of time with music.'

Fortunately for the band, they were caught up in the movement at its healthiest stage, and ironically ended up spearheading a sound that in reality they wanted little part of at the outset. Mark once put their playing down to being like an engine firing on four cylinders. Their talent lies in a spontaneous creativity, perfecting an infectious groove that is both soothing and explosive. For some, these precise textures are like supermarket muzak, unsurprising, bland and even comatose. It's an undemanding music with its roots in those early years on the periphery of mainstream chart music, but which was later to strike a resonant chord with the buying public. Their peripatetic lifestyle finally paid off.

Ironically, back in April 1981, Phil Gould told Stephanie Calman for *Black Echoes*: 'It is a business, you know, and you've got to look at it like that. It's unfortunate that sometimes you lose the artistic side of music because of that. But if you want to play music for your own enjoyment you have to at least – not contrive the records – but have some sort of saleability. And that's not a particularly bad thing. I don't mind, and I know what goes on. And if we can have something to sell records by, we can also show our personalities through those records and develop something of our own.'

Level 42 have indeed been called many things, and some of the more caustic remarks, however undeserved, have undoubtedly stung. Even today, to many people the band are regarded as faceless. But then, to be fair, they have accepted that all along.

For Mark King and Mike Lindup, they are now content to take time off the road, away from the crowds. Relaxing in his new studio, Mark says: 'I just want to work all the time at writing and making music. I can sit here and get really self-indulgent and do whatever takes my fancy.'

Discography

The Singles

Love Meeting Love/Instrumental Love
Elite Dazz 5
Released April 1980

Love Meeting Love/Instrumental Love
Polydor POSP 170
Released 4 August 1980

(Flying On The) Wings Of Love/Wings Of Love
Polydor POSP 200
Released 11 November 1980

Love Games/42
Polydor POSP 234
Released 23 March 1981

Turn It On/Beezer One
Polydor POSP 286
Released 20 July 1981

Starchild/Foundation And Empire Parts 1 and 2
Polydor POSP 343
Released 19 October 1981

Are You Hearing (What I Hear)/The Return of the Handsome Rugged Man
Polydor POSP 396
Released 22 April 1982

Weave Your Spell/Love Games (live)
Polydor POSP 500
Released 17 September 1982

The Chinese Way/88 (live)
Polydor POSP 538
Released 4 January 1983

Out of Sight, Out of Mind/You Can't Blame Louis
Polydor POSOP 570
Released 31 March 1983

Out of Sight, Out of Mind/You Can't Blame Louis (picture disc)
Polydor POSP 570
Released 31 March 1983

The Sun Goes Down (Living It Up)/Can't Walk You Home
Polydor POSP 622
Released 14 July 1983

The Sun Goes Down (Living It Up)/Can't Walk You Home (cassette)
Polydor POSMC 622
Released 4 August 1983

Micro Kid/Turn It On (live)
Polydor POSP 643
Released 6 October 1983

Standing In The Light/Love Meeting Love
Polydor POSP 663
Released November 1983

Hot Water/Standing in the Light (remix)
Polydor POSP 697
Released 16 August 1984

The Chant Has Begun (edited version)/**Almost There** (edited version)
Polydor POSP 710
Released 17 October 1984

The Chant Has Begun/**Love Games** (US remix)/**Almost There/The Sun Goes Down**
Polydor POSPA 710
Released 1 November 1984

Standing in the Light/Love Meeting Love
Polydor POSPA 697
Released 14 March 1985

A Physical Presence (EP): **Follow Me/Turn It On/Kansas City Milkman/Mr Pink** (all live)
Polydor POSP 746
Released 30 May 1985

Something About You/Coup D'Etat
Polydor POSP 759
Released 5 September 1985

Something About You/Coup D'Etat (sleeve)
Polydor POSPG 759
Released 16 September 1985

Something About You/Coup D'Etat (10″)
Polydor POSPT 759
Released 16 October 1985

Leaving Me Now/I Sleep on My Heart
Polydor POSP 776
Released 31 October 1985

Leaving Me Now/I Sleep on My Heart (10″)
Polydor POSPT 776
Released 31 October 1985

Leaving Me Now/I Sleep on My Heart/Coup D'Etat/Leaving Me Now
(doublepack single)
Polydor POSPD 776
Released 11 December 1985

Lessons in Love/Hot Water (live)
Polydor POSP 790
Released 10 April 1986

Running in the Family/Dream Crazy
Polydor POSP 842
Released 29 January 1987

To Be with You Again/Micro Kid (live)
Polydor POSP 855
Released 8 April 1987

To Be with You Again/Micro Kid (picture disc)
Polydor POSPP 855
Released 11 May 1987

It's Over (remix)/Physical Presence **(live)**
Polydor POSP 900
Released 26 August 1987

It's Over (extended)/**Physical Presence** (live)/**It's Over** (instrumental) (cassette)
Polydor POSPC 900
Released 27 August 1987

It's Over/Physical Presence (gatefold sleeve)
Polydor POSPG 900
Released 14 September 1987

Children Say/Starchild
Polydor POSP 911
Released 25 November 1987

Children Say (extended remix)/**Starchild** (remix)/**Children Say/Something About You** (cassette)
Polydor POSPC 911
Released 1 December 1987

Children Say (remix)/**Starchild** (remix) [picture disc]
Polydor POSPP 911
Released 7 December 1987

Children Say/Starchild/Children Say (platinum edition remix) (CD single)
Polydor POCD 911
Released 9 December 1987

Heaven in My Hands/Gresham Blues
Polydor PO14
Released 17 August 1988

Heaven in My Hands (CDS)
Polydor PZCD 14
Released 24 August 1988

Take a Look/Man
Polydor PZ24
Released 12 October 1988

Take a Look/Man/Take a Look (extended) (CDS)
Polydor PZCD24
Released 19 October 1988

Tracie/Three Words
Polydor PO34
Released 5 January 1989

Tracie (extended remix)/**Three Words**
POG34
Released 5 January 1989

Tracie/Three Words/Tracie (extended) CDS
Polydor PZCD34
Released 11 January 1989

12″ Singles

Love Meeting Love/Instrumental Love
Elite DAZZ 5
Released April 1980

Love Meeting Love/Instrumental Love
Polydor POSPX 170
Released 4 August 1980

(Flying on the) Wings of Love/Wings of Love
Polydor POSPX 200
Released 10 November 1980

Love Games/42
Polydor POSPX 234
Released 23 March 1981

Turn It On/Beezer One
Polydor POSPX 286
Released 20 July 1981

Starchild (remix)/**Foundation And Empire Parts 1 and 2**
Polydor POSPX 343
Released 19 October 1981

Are You Hearing (What I Hear)/The Return of the Handsome Rugged Man
Polydor POSPX 396
Released 22 April 1982

Weave Your Spell/Love Games (live)/**Dune Tune** (live)
Polydor POSPX 500
Released 17 September 1982

The Chinese Way/88 (live)
Polydor POSPX 538
Released 4 January 1983

Out of Sight, Out of Mind/You Can't Blame Louis (remix)
Polydor POSPX 570
Released 31 March 1983

Out of Sight, Out of Mind/You Can't Blame Louis (picture disc)
Polydor POPPX570
Released 5 May 1983

The Sun Goes Down (Living It Up)/Can't Walk You Home
Polydor POSPX 622
Released 14 July 1983

Micro Kid/Turn It On (live)
Polydor POSPX 643
Released 6 October 1983

Micro Kid/The Chinese Way
Polydor POSXX 643
Released 25 October 1983

Standing in the Light/Love Meeting Love
Polydor POSPX 663
Released November 1983

Hot Water/Standing in the Light (remix)
Polydor POSPX 697
Released 16 August 1984

The Chant Has Begun (power mix)/**Almost There/The Sun Goes Down**
(upfront mix)
Polydor POSPX 710
Released 17 October 1984

A Physical Presence (EP): **Follow Me/Turn It On/Kansas City Milkman/Mr
Pink** (all live)
Polydor POSPX 746
Released 30 May 1985

Something About You/Coup D'Etat (version)
Polydor POSPX 759
Released 5 September 1985

Something About You (Sisa mix)/**Coup D'Etat** (version)/**Hot Water/The Sun Goes Down**
Polydor POSPA 759
Released 26 September 1985

Leaving Me Now/I Sleep On My Heart/Leaving Me Now/Dream Crazy
Polydor POSPX 776
Released 31 October 1985

Lessons in Love/World Machine/Hot Water (live)
Polydor POSPX 790
Released 10 April 1986

Lessons In Love/Something About You (U.S. remix)/**Hot Water** (live)
Polydor POSPA 790
Released 6 September 1986

Running in the Family (extended)/**Dream Crazy/Running in the Family** (7″ 8 version)
Polydor POSPX 842
Released 21 January 1987

Running in the Family (extended)/**Dream Crazy/Running in the Family** (7″ 8 version)/**Lessons in Love/Children Say/It's Over** (doublepack)
Polydor POSPXX 842
Released 16 February 1987

To Be with You Again/Micro Kid/Lessons in Love
Polydor POSPX 855
Released 8 April 1987

To Be with You Again (ADSC mix)/**To Be with You Again** (dub)/**Micro Kid** (live)
Polydor POSPA 855
Released 29 April 1987

It's Over (extended remix)/**Physical Presence** (live)/**It's Over** (instrumental)
Polydor POSPX 900
Released 26 August 1987

It's Over (remix)/**Physical Presence** (live)/**Running in the Family** (remix)
Polydor POSPA 900
Released 21 September 1987

Children Say/Starchild
Polydor POSPX 911
Released 25 November 1987

Heaven in My Hands (remix)/**Heaven in My Hands** (7″) **Gresham Blues**
8 Polydor PZ14
Released 17 August 1988

Heaven in My Hands (US remix)/**Heaven in My Hands** (7″) **Gresham Blues**
Polydor PZX14
Released 5 September 1988

Take a Look (extended)/**Man/Take a Look** (7″)
Polydor PZ24
Released 12 October 1988

Take a Look (extended)/**Man/Take a Look** (7″)
Polydor PZY24
Released 31 October 1988

Tracie (extended)/**Tracie** (7″)/**Three Words**
Polydor PZ34
Released 5 January 1989

Tracie (US remix)/**Tracie** (7″)/**Three Words**
Polydor PZX34
Released 18 January 1989

Albums

LEVEL 42
LP: POLS 1036 (Released: 13 July 1981)
MC: POLSC 1036 (29 May 1981)
CD: 821 9352 (16 March 1987)

Turn It On
43
Why Are You Leaving
Almost There
Heathrow
Love Games
Dune Tune
Starchild

THE EARLY TAPES – JULY/AUGUST 1980
LP: SPELP 28 (4 August 1983)
MC: SPEMC 28 (4 August 1983)

Sandstorm
Love Meeting Love
Theme to Margaret
Mr Pink
Autumn (Paradise Is Free)
Wings of Love
Woman
88

THE PURSUIT OF ACCIDENTS
LP: POLD 5067 (3 September 1982)
MC: POLDC 5067 (3 September 1982)
CD: 810 0152 (28 February 1985)

Weave Your Spell
The Pursuit of Accidents
Last Chance
Are You Hearing (What I Hear)
You Can't Blame Louis
Eyes Waterfalling
Shapeshifter
The Chinese Way

STANDING IN THE LIGHT
LP: POLD 5110 (18 August 1983)
MC: POLDC 5110 (18 August 1983)
CD: 813 8652 (17 November 1983)

Micro Kid
Sun Goes Down (Living It Up)
Out of Sight, Out of Mind
Dance on Heavy Weather
A Pharaohs Dream
Standing in the Light
I Want Eyes
People
The Machine Stops

INFLUENCES – MARK KING'S SOLO ALBUM
LP: MKLP1 (5 July 1984)
MC: MKMC1 (5 July 1984)
CD: 823 0882 (5 July 1984)

Influences
Clocks Go Forward
I Feel Free
Pictures on the Wall
There Is a Dog

TRUE COLOURS
LP: POLH 10 (27 September 1984)
MC: POLHC 10 (27 September 1984)
CD: 823 5422 (22 November 1984)

The Chant Has Begun
Kansas City Milkman
Seven Days
Hot Water
A Floating Life
True Believers
Kouyate
Hours by the Window My Hero (extra cassette track)

A PHYSICAL PRESENCE
LP: POLH 23 (19 June 1985)
MC: POLHC 23 (19 June 1985)
CD: 825 6772 (29 July 1985)

Almost There
Turn It On
Mr Pink
Eyes Waterfalling
Kansas City Milkman
Follow Me
Foundation and Empire
The Chant Has Begun
The Chinese Way
The Sun Goes Down (Living It Up)
Hot Water
Love Games
88

WORLD MACHINE
LP: POLH 25 (9 October 1985)
MC: POLHC 25 (9 October 1985)
CD: 827 4872 (28 October 1985)

World Machine
Physical Presence
Something About You
Leaving Me Now
I Sleep on My Heart
It's Not the Same for Us
Good Man in a Storm
Coup D'Etat
Lying Still

RUNNING IN THE FAMILY
LP: POLH 42 (11 March 1987)
MC: POLHC 42 (11 March 1987)
CD: 831 5932 (11 March 1987)

Lessons in Love
Children Say
Running in the Family
It's Over
To Be with You Again
Two Solitudes
Fashion Fever
The Sleepwalkers

STARING AT THE SUN
LP: POLH 50 (14 September 1988)
MC: POLHC 50 (14 September 1988)
CD: 837 2472 (14 September 1988)

Heaven in My Hands
I Don't Know Why
Take a Look
Over There
Silence
Tracie
Staring at the Sun
Two Hearts Collide
Man
Gresham Blues (cassette and CD only)